DERBY
PAST & PRESENT

MAXWELL CRAVEN

The History Press

First published in 2004 by
Sutton Publishing Limited

Reprinted in 2017 by
The History Press
The Mill, Brimscombe Port,
Stroud, Gloucestershire, GL5 2QG
www.thehsitorypress.co.uk

Title page photograph: The Old Mayor's
Parlour, a timber-framed elite town house of

1487 destroyed by the borough council in 1948. This
postcard is signed R. Keene (Jr). *(Author)*

British Library Cataloguing in Publication Data
A catalogue record for this book is available from the
British Library.

ISBN 0-7509-4010-7

Typeset in 10.5/13.5 Photina.
Typesetting and origination by
Sutton Publishing Limited.
Printed and bound in England.

Derby Civic Society

Derby Civic Society was founded in 1961 to stimulate public interest in the built and natural environment of the City. It seeks to secure the preservation, protection, benign development, and improvement of any features of beauty, historic importance, architectural interest or public esteem within the City's boundaries.

It also acts as a co-ordinating body, ensuring co-operation, wherever possible, between the Planning and Development Sub-committee of the City Council, of other relevant statutory bodies, industrial or voluntary organisations as well as kindred bodies and persons having aims similar to those for the Society.

The Society acts as a sponsor of, and a channel for, the latest research affecting the history and heritage of the City and its surrounding area, the better to make aware those in whose hands decisions about the future of historic buildings and landscapes lie.

The Society also seeks to take a pro-active role in gaining statutory protection for threatened buildings and landscapes, in identifying possible threats and attempting to bring any concerns likely to arise to the attention of the relevant authorites. A newsletter is published twice yearly and monthly meetings for members, both social and informative, are organised.

The Society is currently lobbying for a complete revision of the Statutory List in Derby, for a solution to the problem of St Helen's House, a grade 1 listed 18th century town house, long on English Heritage's Buildings at Risk Register, and to ameliorate the disastrous effects of the current extensions to the Derby Inner Ring Road in association with two other local amenity societies, Derby HEART and the Derby Heritage Society.

The Society includes both individual and corporate members and is always keen to expand membership. Further information and a membership application form may be obtained from Robin Wood Esq., 103 Whitaker Road, Derby (01332 342321).

CONTENTS

Derby from the east, *c.* 1818. This is taken from a painted Derby Porcelain plaque by William Corden (1797–1867). The three churches of All Saints, St Michael and St Alkmund still dominate the slightly hazy looking horizon, but are rather upstaged by William Cox & Sons' 149ft high shot tower in Tenant Street (1809, demolished 1932) and, far left, William Strutt's six-storey 'fireproof' calico mill of 1793 (demolished 1876, ironically after suffering two fires). Even at this late date the orchards and gardens on the east side of the river – where Erasmus Darwin had a pleasure ground – largely survived, although they were about to succumb to a new suburb called Canary Island. *(Neales, Derby)*

An anonymous painting of Derby in the late seventeenth century, now at Renishaw Hall. It was probably produced for a member of the Sacheverell family, whose house is on the extreme left of the view. The house in the centre is Exeter House (demolished 1854) where on 4–6 December 1745 Bonnie Prince Charlie stayed. All Saints' tower (now Derby Cathedral) is right of centre, with the house of Britain's first Astronomer Royal, John Flamsteed, visible with its tall lantern between the towers of St Michael and (right) St Alkmund. At the river's edge, between St Michael's and Flamsteed House, are the wheels of George Sorocold's water lifting engine of 1691, which gave Derby its first water supply, lasting until 1848. *(Sir Reresby Sitwell Bt)*

PREFACE

Derby is fortunate in having had among its citizens Richard Keene (1825–94), who assiduously photographed the streets of the Borough from 1853 until his death. His earlier pictures, mainly taken in the 1850s, show Derby barely altered since the eighteenth century, a record few British towns can match. He also catalogued the beginning of the changes that sought to improve the town in the later nineteenth century. His successors and rivals continued his work, and in the years after the Second World War, when far-reaching plans were being implemented, the transformation of Derby was recorded.

Over the past six years I have been fortunate enough to acquire three collections of Keene's work, including several views never previously seen and others never published, giving me a modest archive on which to draw. I might add that in each case, having had copies made, I have passed the collection on to Derby Museum at cost to add to a collection that, even in my time, ran to over 13,000 photographs of the city taken over 150 years.

Thus, in this book, there have been several instances where I have selected a Keene view, an Edwardian view and then a more recent view, for nearly everywhere in the city centre there have been multiple and often significant changes.

Elsewhere, Derby has been blessed with a large number of outstanding buildings and, although many have been lost to municipal vandalism or the expediency of the developer, far more remain than one might normally expect in an industrial city of a quarter of a million inhabitants. Therefore, this book also looks at changes to individual buildings and their sites as well as general streetscapes, in its quest for contrast.

Neither do I make apology for pointing the finger of blame where I feel that seriously deleterious changes have come about or commenting – entirely subjectively – on what I see as alterations that have been destructive or simply unnecessary. Derby's elected representatives and those who serve them have, on the whole, showed a marked lack of appreciation for the diversity and distinction of the city's built environment; I see no reason to spare any blushes they might have.

Since ancient times architecture has been regarded as one of the arts, yet if we treated paintings or sculpture as we treat fine buildings, there would be precious little great art left to enjoy. Politicians tend to forget (if they ever knew) that fine buildings in their proper setting can have the same effect as great art in other media: to uplift the spirit, refresh the mind and improve the quality of life. A decent building (like a decent painting) doesn't have to be of the first rank to satisfy and makes its own unique contribution to the *genius loci*, even if we do not know who was responsible for its creation. And if some person of local or national renown has a connection with a particular building it is thereby enriched, and by such increments of history so are we.

What follows, then, may contain elements of criticism, but it also celebrates Derby and its heritage. It is just that such a heritage must be understood as both precious, fragile and largely irreplaceable; that way we can all become involved in helping to protect it.

Maxwell Craven
Derby, June 2004

ACKNOWLEDGEMENTS

Much of the research that has gone into the captions that follow was accumulated over thirty years, and I thus owe a debt of gratitude to all my former colleagues at Derby Museum, many of those who have told me things I didn't know, and especially to the staff, past and present, of the Derby Local Studies Library, who have always been so tolerant and helpful.

My heartfelt thanks for the loan of pictures and for information are due to so many friends and acquaintances as well as those kind people who read my twice-weekly historical column in the *Derby Evening Telegraph* and have volunteered pictures and information in prodigious quantities. If the following list – as seems likely – is not complete, then to anyone omitted I submit my most abject apologies: Michael Allseybrook of Ashton Antiques, Peter Billson, Alan Champion, James Darwin, Don Farnsworth, David Fraser and his colleagues at the Derby Museum, Olga Fraser, Frank Gilbert, Don Gwinnett, the late Roy Hughes, Robert Innes-Smith, Derek Jewell, Nigel Kirk, James Lewis, Roger Pegg, Gerald Redfern, Rose Robinson, Sir Reresby Sitwell Bt, Sheila Tarling, Michael Willis and Peggy Withington.

I am also most grateful to my colleagues at the *Derby Evening Telegraph* for always being so helpful, even though I hardly ever see them! Finally, to my wife Carole, for forbearance, tolerance, the application to my needs of her superb driving skills and her critical eye, for all of which I am in her debt and to whom I offer my thanks and appreciation.

INTRODUCTION

History

Derby was founded (according to the latest research) in about 921 by King Edward the Elder as a Saxon *burh* and equipped with a minster church, which was also a Royal Free Chapel (now the cathedral church of All Saints) and a mint. The latter issued coin until 1154. Prior to 921 the future site of Derby included an earlier minster church, later dedicated to the Northumbrian Prince-martyr St Alkmund, which served a large area bounded by the Trent, Dove and Erewash then called Northworthy. This was suppressed (or nearly so) by the Danes from 874. The Danes, in their turn, refortified the walls of the nearby former Roman small town of Derventio (now Little Chester and always within Derby's boundaries) before being ejected by Queen Aethelflaeda of Mercia in 917.

In 1086 the borough contained 153 burgesses and was also served by at least eight parish churches, while a little later six monastic establishments were founded. It was first granted a charter in about 1155, and numerous others subsequently until 1682, each conferring additional privileges, the Mayoralty being established by one of 1637. Until 1959 Derby was the county town and the focus of the county's chief markets.

Derby's hinterland was extremely rich and the county's landowners unusually opulent, mainly through the exploitation of natural resources including coal and lead ore (galena). The wealthy spent their money in Derby, building numerous fine town residences (of which a number survive) and encouraging industries and crafts that catered for what one might term the luxury end of the market: pewter, gloves, silver, wrought iron (including England's greatest native-born wrought-iron smith, Robert Bakewell (1682–1752), who trained under Jean Tijou at Hampton Court), clocks and so on. In 1718 this upmarket trend was reinforced when the Derby Silk Mill began production under Sir Thomas and John Lombe, arguably Britain's first factory, with all the processes of manufacture under one roof, all powered by a common source – the Derwent.

Later other silk mills were established, as well as cotton and calico mills, by Jedediah Strutt and his kin the Evans family. Indeed, the cotton mills established by the latter at Darley Abbey in 1782 are the best preserved in the Derwent Valley and the centrepiece (with the rebuilt Silk Mill) of the Derwent Valley World Heritage Site. The village of Darley Abbey itself must be one of the best preserved Regency industrial villages in the UK.

Another luxury industry was established in about 1750 when William Duesbury and Andre Planche began porcelain production, which has gone on in the city without

Derby Silk Mill, from the river, painting by Moses Griffiths, 1774. On the left is the island, which was home to John Lombe's garden and monument, and the weir, then recently completed by the architect Joseph Pickford. *(Derby Museum)*

interruption ever since. Even when iron founding began in the late eighteenth century it was initially to supply architectural decorative features for grand houses under the stimulus of Robert Adam's Kedleston (where it was used extensively), and it was not until the early nineteenth century that the foundries diversified into less glamorous products.

The coming of the railway in 1839 led the foundry industry into heavy engineering, although Rolls-Royce, the last foundry to open in Derby in 1908, started off as a manufacturer of prestige motor cars, thus continuing this 'luxury industries' tradition. However, car production stopped with the outbreak of the Second World War and the firm is now world-renowned as a maker of aero-engines, an element of diversification forced upon Sir Henry Royce by the requirements of the First World War. Surviving luxury industries are porcelain (Royal Crown Derby) and turret clock-making (John Smith & Sons).

Clock-making was transformed locally from 1736 when the eminent scientist, mechanician and polymath John Whitehurst FRS (1713–88) set up in Derby in the trade. By the later 1750s he was on close terms with Erasmus Darwin FRS and Matthew Boulton, and by 1764 was a founder member, with them, of the Lunar Society. Although today an undeservedly largely forgotten figure, he was important as the father of modern geology, a pioneer of the flushing loo, of kitchen equipment, especially roasters and stoves, the back-boiler, domestic heating and modern plumbing generally, latter of which he pioneered with the encouragement of the

2nd Duke of Newcastle at Clumber Park, Notts. The Duke, who became a close friend, ultimately obtained for him a sinecure at the Royal Mint in 1774. Whitehurst left Derby permanently for London in 1780, where he later developed a device for measuring 100ths of a second and another to arrive at a constant and standard unit of measure from which a universal system (and decimal) of mensuration could be derived. Had he not died in 1788, he might have brought a decimal system to Britain a decade before this was achieved in France.

As Whitehurst left Derby so Darwin arrived, taking up residence at 3 Full Street in 1783 and dying at nearby Breadsall Priory in 1802, after revolutionising many aspects of science and promoting it through his didactic poetry. He and his Lunar Society colleagues, along with Derby's most opulent private citizen, the Revd Thomas Gisborne

Portrait of John Whitehurst FRS by his friend Joseph Wright of Derby ARA, *c.* 1782. *(John Smith & Sons, Derby)*

of St Helen's House, were at the spearhead of Wilberforce's campaign to end slavery within HM's dominions. Both Boulton and Wedgwood (another Lunar Society friend) struck versions of the famous medallion 'Am I not a man and a brother?' in bronze and Jasper-ware at this time. Gisborne, it might be added, was the last and most influential patron of Derby's eighteenth-century artist Joseph Wright ARA (1734–97), who painted portraits of many of the influential Midlanders of his age and created unmatched scientific set-pieces such as *A Philosopher Lecturing upon an Orrery, An Experiment with a Bird in an Air Pump* and *Cromford Mill by Night.*

Darwin's protégés included William Strutt FRS (1756–1831), who took many of his revolutionary ideas forward into the industrial age he and his friends had helped to create. These included his ground-breaking educational ideas, all of which long-anticipated modern methods, and were put into practice by his friend Matthew Spencer, and in due course influenced his son, the Derby-born philosopher and proto-sociologist, Herbert Spencer (1820–1903). With his death, a 250-year cycle of scientific achievement in Derby, initiated by John Flamsteed FRS, from 1675 England's first Astronomer Royal, and sustained by Whitehurst and his associates, came to an end.

The nineteenth century saw the transformation of Derby into a leading industrial town, but one that boasted the UK's first public park (donated by Joseph Strutt in

1840) and the third ever UK Co-operative Society, founded in 1850. The era of philosophy and luxury goods gave way to one of iron and narrow tapes, of railways, forges and feverish expansion. Yet within that girdle of industry the historic core of the town remained intact, its markets still meeting the needs of the county's farmers and estates and its medieval street pattern and buildings preserved.

The predilection of Hertfordshire-born printer and bookseller Richard Keene (1823–94) for photography, encouraged by W.H. Fox-Talbot's friend Canon Edward Abney of The Firs, meant that from autumn 1853 (the occasion of his first datable surviving photographic image) Keene assiduously recorded the town's streets and buildings. This valuable record was continued by his third son, Charles Barrow Keene, until 1931 and by increasing numbers of other imitators, encouraged by the success of the Derby Photographic Society of which Keene was a co-founder.

Just as Keene began recording the town its medieval streets were beginning to be widened, a process that began with Iron Gate in 1866 and ended with Full Street in the

A Keene view looking north from Corn Market to Rotten Row and Iron Gate, showing a corner of the Piazzas, May 1855. *(Author)*

1930s. Thus a full series of 'before and after' views of most streets can be assembled to catalogue this first phase in the modernisation of the borough.

After the Second World War an iconoclastic elected gerontocracy, heedless of Derby's then virtually intact built environment, set about the destruction of much that was deemed ancient or passé and its replacement by buildings that were of indifferent quality even by the aesthetically arid standards of the time. This process was accelerated by the building in 1967–9 of part of a projected inner ring road, which destroyed the town's only Georgian square, a fine nineteenth-century church by H.I. Stevens (albeit revealing, in the archaeology of its site, much that was previously but poorly understood of the settlement's early history) and several other buildings of merit. That an adjacent railway line, along the alignment of which the entire enterprise could easily have been pitched, was then on the point of closure was, in the event, but a tragic coda to the whole lamentable business.

The ring road's continuation, now under way, appears likely to isolate the centre of the city (a status conferred in 1977), compromise the setting of St Helen's House, destroy Richard Brown's pioneering marble works opposite, render useless on a traffic island the late seventeenth-century timber-framed Seven Stars inn and affect the integrity of the area's premier conservation area, Friar Gate.

By the mid-twentieth century there was much to be proud of. The Central Improvement Plan of 1931, although curtailed by the war, showed that visionary planning and decent architecture could go hand in hand. Derby also has an extraordinarily large number of public parks, some of exceptional quality, although the gerontocracy's readiness to demolish the Georgian mansions that provided the focus of two of them (both laid out by local man William Emes) and to neglect criminally a third serves as a reminder of the basic incompatibility of local authorities and historic buildings.

Yet the basic conservatism of this same clique meant that the bandwagon of the tower block was not, in the 1960s, leapt upon and consequently, although the city has three relatively 'high-rise' buildings, none blight the skyline and there are no high-rise estates ringing the city; a notable achievement by any standard. Recently, however, a nine-storey block of flats (now euphemistically referred to as 'apartments') has received planning and conservation area consent for erection on the river's bank beside Thomas Harrison's St Mary's Bridge (1794), opposite the tower of the Silk Mill (1821) and vying for attention with the late Perpendicular tower of the cathedral, completed in 1532.

Nevertheless, these two basic eras of drastic change in Derby's environment – the second half of the nineteenth and the second half of the twentieth centuries – have led to an *embarras de richesse* in the material available to provide contrasts in this book, even discounting the fact that the sheer and commendable voracity of local people for profusely illustrated books about their city rather limits the choice of image if excessive repetition is to be avoided.

Also in the last fifty years, as its traditional industries have declined, Derby has been able to replace them by successfully diversifying into hi-tech, electronic and service industries which have maintained its trading base and prosperity into the present millennium.

Derby from Abbey Barns, by Thomas Hofland and recently acquired for Derby Museum, *c.* 1807. *(Christies)*

Architectural Heritage

For a mainly industrial city of a quarter of a million inhabitants, Derby's architectural heritage is unexpectedly rich, despite the depredations of the last century. A hint that this should be so emerges from the complimentary accounts of many travellers, from Celia Fiennes through Daniel Defoe – 'A town of Gentry rather than trade' – to Joseph Farington RA, William Mavor and Sir Richard Philips. All commend its fine appearance, spacious and elegant Market Place and good brick buildings. Even, grudgingly, the hyper-critical Lord Torrington had some good words to say.

Although the statutory list has not been revised for twenty-five years and is probably quite thirty or forty entries short were it brought up to date, it still has 274 separate entries, of which 6 are grade I listed, 2 churches grade A, and 28 grade II*. Listings are given within brackets without comment in the captions that follow. Of the churches, the best medieval ones are in the suburbs, notably St Mary at Chaddesden of mid-fourteenth-century date, St Werburgh at Spondon of similar date (and both mainly built within a generation), followed by All Saints' at Mickleover, St Peter's at Chellaston and St Peter's in the city centre, albeit that the last was rebuilt twice in the nineteenth century. Of paramount importance is the chapel of St Mary-on-the-Bridge dating from about 1440, one of only six bridge chapels to survive in the UK. By far and away the most striking church is James Gibbs's All Saints' (1723–5), since 1927 Derby's cathedral and sensitively extended in 1969–71 by Sebastian Comper, along with A.W.N. Pugin's majestic Catholic Church of St Mary (1838–44).

The city has two fine late medieval houses, most notably Stone House Prebend, Little Chester, and over a dozen dating from the earlier seventeenth century. These include the timber-framed 22 Iron Gate and Mickleover Old Hall, the elaborate brick Jacobean House, Wardwick, and 48 Sadler Gate, not forgetting the grand town house of the Gells of Hopton, 16 Friar Gate; more lurk behind later façades. From later in that century the city has a whole run of town houses and burghers' residences in Classical style (the best being Franceys' House, 3–5 Market Place), as well as the vernacular Old Bell Hotel, Sadler Gate, which contains the finest oak staircase of the period.

The greatest public building in Derby is also from this period: the 1659–60 Shire Hall by George Eaton of Etwall. This is flanked by the former King's Arms County Hotel of 1798 and the Judges' Lodgings (by John Welch of Derby, 1809–11) forming a most impressive *cour d'honneur* and without doubt the finest legal complex in the Midlands excepting only Lincoln Castle. The Shire Hall was added to in 1772 by Joseph Pickford and extensively by Matthew Habershon in 1828 (assisted by William and George Strutt), producing an important ensemble. The structure has been rather drastically

The Shire Hall (I) in its heyday, seen here with the carriage, trumpeters and pikemen of High Sheriff Col Godfrey Mosley of Calke Abbey, 1931. *(Roger Pegg Esq.)*

Robert Wallace's Royal Hotel, Athenaeum (II) and bank on the Victoria Street/Corn Market corner, just prior to pedestrianisation, July 1990. *(Author)*

altered recently by conversion into the city's new magistrates' courts, involving the loss of Habershon's extensions and the provision of some rather inadequate new build, bearing in mind that they were added to a grade I listed building in a conservation area.

All decades of the eighteenth century are represented, the most striking ensembles being in St Mary's Gate, Wardwick and lower Friar Gate. Derby produced an exceptionally fine architect of the later eighteenth century in Joseph Pickford (1734–82) who designed for many of the Lunar Society, was clerk of works for Robert Adam at Kedleston and was a close friend of the local luminaries of the eighteenth century. Although some of his Derby buildings have unfortunately been lost, his own house of 1769 (41 Friar Gate, now a museum) and three others nearby, along with his former Tiger Inn, Corn Market (1764), survive.

Most important of all is Pickford's St Helen's House, King Street, designed and built in 1766–7 and accepted as the finest Palladian town house outside London. Unfortunately, thirty years of neglect has led to its being shut up and earmarked for sale, despite vociferous opposition, some of it from people of the selfsame ideological standpoint of those elected representatives who allowed it to sink into its present parlous state in the first place.

During the Regency period industry experienced difficulties because of the diminishing amount of land available, and by a series of Acts of Parliament from 1768 four successive Improvement Commissions were established to raise a rate

The former General Post Office, Victoria Street (II), of 1861–7, by J. Williams, 1997. (*Author*)

and overhaul the city's failing infrastructure. Three were chaired from 1792 to 1829 by William Strutt FRS (1756–1830) of St Helen's House and gave Derby a series of very striking Regency townscapes, notably the Royal Hotel, Athenaeum, bank and post office, on the Corn Market/Victoria Street corner (Robert Wallace, 1836–9), Vernon Street and the County Gaol (Francis Goodwin, 1826–8), St Mary's Bridge (Thomas Harrison of Chester, 1789–94) and North Parade (William Smith, 1819–21).

At the same time some fine mills were built to complement the 1718 Silk Mill (rebuilt after a fire in 1910), notably the Rykneild (silk) Mills of 1811, now tastefully converted into 'apartments'. There are also a number of particularly fine stuccoed villas in the suburbs – most still unlisted, with three recently demolished or wrecked and one long abandoned and under threat. Nevertheless, The Pastures (now the Boys' Grammar School), Littleover, is particularly fine, as are Highfields (1826), The Leylands (1819) and Parkfield (1821).

In the Victorian era many of the city's large public buildings were erected, beginning with the rebuilding of the Guildhall by Derby-born Henry Duesbury (1842). The most elegant are without doubt the former GPO (J. Williams, 1861) and the Standing Order inn, formerly Crompton & Evans's Union Bank (J. Chatwin of Birmingham, 1880); both are exquisitely proportioned essays in Italian Palazzo revival, and the banking hall of the latter has been acknowledged as the finest to survive in the region.

The Museum and Art Gallery (R.K. Freeman and J.S. Storey, 1879–82), Wardwick, constitute a fine ensemble in the William Burges mould. The Strand, Strand Arcade, Wardwick corner and St James's Street (Giles & Brookhouse with G.H. Sheffield, 1878–81) constitute the best surviving Victorian townscaping.

The finest local architect of the period was Henry Isaac Stevens (1806–73), who was trained by Sir Jeffrey Wyatville and William Martin of Bretby. Some of his Derby buildings have gone, but the former Temperance Hall (1853), Diocesan Training College (1852) and a number of shops in Iron Gate (1866–75) remain. His partner F.J. Robinson (died 1893) designed the finest of all late Victorian Houses, Darley Slade in Duffield Road (1891). This street is a nearly unspoilt later Victorian set-piece full of important houses ranging from the Regency period to the 1930s, including a small villa by Barry Parker and Sir Raymond Unwin. F.W. Waller of Gloucester and Thomas Simmonds built the arresting Technical College (1882), Green Lane, in an Arts and Crafts Gothic style.

The Arts and Crafts era produced Sir Arthur Blomfield's gifted protégé Percy Heylin Currey (died 1942) whose St Helen's House chapel and a number of private residences, as well as two other churches, still grace the city. Of the latter, the soaring brick St Osmund (1902), Osmaston, is without doubt the finest of its date in the region, set within a collegiate-style quadrangle of ancillary buildings of immense charm.

Even in the interwar period Derby was well served by its architects, notably the Eatons (father and son), Bernard Widdows and Herbert Aslin. The latter (died 1959) was borough architect 1929–45 and produced a whole series of exceptionally fine buildings, mostly as part of the Central Improvement Plan, which sought to replace older industries from the town centre beside the Derwent and impose a 'municipal quarter' of some elegance.

Although elements of this are about to be lost to a redevelopment scheme (including his innovative, parabolically planned, bus station), the recently spotlisted magistrates' courts and police station are least altered with fine period interiors. Nevertheless, there are pleasing examples of his 108 known works scattered around the city in a variety of styles ranging from the epic, like the Classical council house, to an attractive *Moderne* bowls pavilion on Normanton Park. A final notable building of this era is the former Aiton's Works, Stores Road, of 1932 (recently spotlisted courtesy of Derby Civic Society, which has been instrumental in adding eighteen buildings to the list since

St Osmund's Church, Osmaston, 2001. *(Author)*

Aslin's allusive ordinary bicycle on a metal gate, municipal baths, on the site of a former cycle shop, Walker Lane, November 1988. *(Author)*

1980). Not only is this a superb *Moderne* building with a landmark interior, but it was designed by two women, Betty Scott and Norah Aiton, daughter of the company's founder, Sir John Aiton.

Aslin was the last architect to have paid great attention to detail in Derby, producing much pleasing metalwork, carved stone plaques and jokey allusions on his buildings. This continued a tradition for which Derby is well known: fine craftsmanship well up to national standards. It is possible to identify the work of individual craftsmen from the early eighteenth century. At that time Derby produced Robert Bakewell, the wrought-iron smith, Samuel Mansfield, Joshua Needham and Abraham Denstone, stuccoists, Jonathan Reading, decorator, Thomas Trimmer and Roger Morledge, joiners, and the Brown dynasty, masons, carvers and later spa turners. These men worked all over England under various architects of national renown, like the Smiths, Talman, Archer and the early Palladians. Their work survives in Derby Cathedral, The Homestead, Spondon and numerous lesser houses in the city. That of their successors in the era of Pickford survives most notably in St Helen's House, where the rich rococo plasterwork is by Abraham Denstone the younger, the ironwork by Bakewell's successor Benjamin Yates, the mason's work by Aeneas Evans and Solomon Brown, and the carving by George Moneypenney (died 1807) and Richard Brown (1735–1816).

Apart from William Emes's parks the other notable Derby landscape is the

Gates to St Mary's Gate House, by Robert Bakewell of about 1732, and moved to Derby
Cathedral after the house was demolished in 1938. The photograph was taken by Richard Keene
on 6 June 1871. *(Author)*

Arboretum (1840) by J.C. Loudon, with attractive buildings by E.B. Lamb and grand
entrance frontispiece by Henry Duesbury (1853) situated on a fine (but run down)
square with houses by C.E. Humphreys of Derby for the Litchurch Local Board (1867).

This tradition of craftsmanship, including that of wrought-iron smithing
(uniquely in a city of iron founders), continued throughout the nineteenth century
and lasted until the Second World War. It is unfortunate that neither the standards
of architecture nor of craftsmanship survived that conflict, most recent building in
the city being banal and meretricious. Nevertheless, compared with other cities it is
by no means as bad as it could have been, nor was the destruction wreaked on the
historic environment from 1961 as serious; exceptional riches remain. One has only
to look at Liverpool, where 18 listed buildings have been demolished over the last
10 months of 2000 and over 100 in the last decade, to realise that Derby (albeit
with a much smaller stock of listed structures) with the loss of less than 30 in
50 years has everything to commend it in this respect.

The architectural heritage of the city, therefore, is exceptional for a manufacturing
centre of its size – one only has to compare the deplorable state of the survival of listed
buildings in Nottingham, Leicester and Sheffield to realise that Derby has much to be
proud of.

1

Market Place, Iron Gate, Queen Street & King Street

A photograph taken by W.W. Winter of Derby Market Place looking north and decorated in honour of the visit of HRH the Prince of Wales to the Royal Agricultural Show on 15 July 1881 at the expense of the Mayor, Alderman Sir Abraham Woodiwiss, a super-rich railway contractor. The Piazzas have not long been knocked down, making the view possible, with the Assembly Rooms (Earl Ferrers, Joseph Pickford and Robert Adam, 1763–74) to the right and Iron Gate leading to All Saints' tower to the left. Archaeology has established that the area around the Market Place was first settled in about 1100. *(Author)*

Nos 2 and 3 Market Place, looking north-east, photographed by Richard Keene, *c.* 1865. The former Virgin's Inn, of about 1709, was rebuilt after a fire of March 1741 and converted by William Cox of Brailsford Hall, lead merchant, into a town house in 1763. A branch of his family later used it as a wine merchants, taken over by Messrs Pountain, and it was replaced in 1889 by a building demolished in 1970 to make way for the present Assembly Rooms. A corner of the previous Assembly Rooms can be seen, right, with Full Street snaking away beside it. *(Author)*

Approximately the same view today. In the foreground the 1923 Cenotaph, designed by Charles Clayton Thompson (1873–1932) of Currey & Thompson and carved by A.G. Walker ARA. The whole area has been subsumed into Sir Hugh Casson's vast, unlovely and over-scale Assembly Rooms (opened 1977) with cavernous car park behind. The stone Palladian façade of the previous Assembly Rooms (II) survived the unnecessary demolition that followed a minor fire of 1963 and was peremptorily dispensed with by Sir Hugh, ending up at Crich Tramway Museum. *(Author)*

A detail from a view of the south side of the Market Place in 1828 by George Pickering. The sumptuous Baroque Guildhall of 1731 features, with a view of Corn Market between it and the south-east angle of the Piazzas of 1708. The architect of the Guildhall was Richard Jackson of Armitage (1703–51), and it was demolished the same year as this view when a plot on the south side became available on which to build afresh. John Whitehurst supplied the clock, earning himself the freedom to trade. *(Derby Museum)*

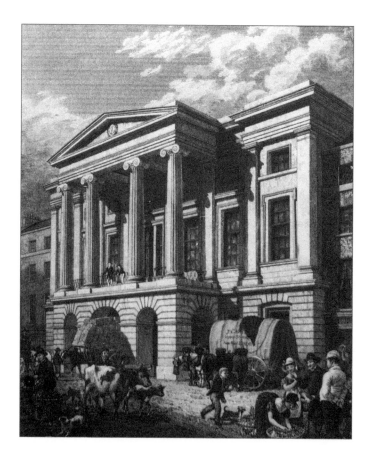

Architect Matthew Habershon's new Guildhall, built 1828–9. Habershon was the favourite architect of the Strutt family, industrialists. This building was destroyed by fire on Trafalgar Day 1841, along with Whitehurst's re-positioned clock. *(Author)*

Above: The new Guildhall (II) and Market Place, 1895. Derby-born architect Henry Duesbury of London designed this building (II) to utilise as much as possible of its predecessor, including almost all of the white-brick south elevation. It ceased to function as a council chamber in 1949, but is an excellent venue for smaller performances and shows. The bas-reliefs are by John Bell (1812–96). Note the Market Place functioning as it was intended. *(Author)*

The Guildhall, May 1992. In 1934 the stalls in the Market Place were succeeded by car parking and then by nothing very much. The double-bowed building to the right was built in 1830 as a replacement Cross Keys inn, but was turned into offices by the *Derbyshire Advertiser* in the 1890s, acquiring an unsympathetic top storey which really ought to be removed. Since 1992 all traffic has been cleared from the area. *(Author)*

Above: The Market Hall (II) photographed by Richard Keene as part of a series in 1864. At this time the hall was ostensibly finished, but the iron structure (made by the Derby founders J. & G. Haywood & Co.) had been found to be of inadequate strength by an official party, seen here inspecting the structure. The borough surveyor who designed it, Robert Thorburn, left suddenly and remedial works were undertaken by his successor, George Thompson, at the cost of the omission of the exterior towers. *(Derby Museum)*

In the 1930s borough architect Herbert Aslin refitted the interior of the Market Hall with new stalls, enabling the council to put up rents. These survived until a further refitting, when more of Thorburn's problems had to be expensively resolved, from 1989 to 1991. Their successors are distinctly inferior. The photograph was taken by Dennis Plowman in 1982. *(Derby Museum)*

Left: The Piazzas, drawn by George Pickering, 1828. From medieval times until 1828 there had been a free-standing Guildhall, and from the sixteenth century a free-standing butchery or shambles on the Market Place's west side. To this (which was simultaneously rebuilt) was added in 1708 The Piazzas, on the east side, financed by banker Samuel Crompton I. Inspired by the Grand Tour and Inigo Jones's Covent Garden, a covered colonnaded walkway gave access for shoppers, with space above for warehousing and workshops. *(Derby Museum)*

Opposite, below: It never really caught on, however, and in 1871 the northern half, along with the Shambles, was demolished, as recorded by Richard Keene in this photograph. The southern half continued in use until the council could afford to buy out the freeholders and demolish it in 1877, clearing the way for the view seen on p. 19. *(Author)*

Below: The same view in June 2004 shows that the 1992 Derby Promenade scheme led to the Market Place becoming cluttered once again, here with street furniture from a French catalogue, inappropriate lights and trees. *(Author)*

Austin's (later Storer's), on the west side of Market Place, photographed by Richard Keene after Rotten Row was demolished, making the view possible, *c.* 1877. This building, with its dentilled timber cornice and Corinthian giant order was built in the 1690s and once had a dormered roof. Stylistically it has much in common with Franceys' House on the left and Lloyd's Bank (see top picture on p. 29), but it is not clear for whom it was built. By 1745, however, it was the town house of the Storers of Kirk Ireton, Mr Storer being host to David Wemyss, Lord Elcho during the 'Forty Five'. *(Author)*

In 1751 Francis Meynell of Anslow acquired the building as an apothecary's shop. In the 1870s it was Storer's grocers, but in 1890 the business was acquired by Giles Austin, as seen here. The date 1796 featured on the timber parapet added by Mr Austin is that of when the grocery business was founded. Austin died in 1929, the business was sold by his heirs and in 1936 this charming house was demolished. *(Author)*.

The replacement building was a rather banal exercise in Classical revival (not helped by its Crittall windows) built in – of all things for a stone-rich county – Portland stone in 1937 for Martin's Bank. Since this firm amalgamated itself out of existence some forty years ago, the building has been the Abbey National. *(Author)*

Smith's Bank and the two buildings next door to Austin's shop to the north photographed by Keene in 1878. Smith's Derby Old Bank was demolished later in 1878. Fley's, the narrow stone Italianate building to the right – about which absolutely nothing is known – survives, albeit with its jolly little dormers removed and a clumsy tripartite top floor substituted. Behind, and through the corridor, lay Mason's (formerly Jolley's) Tap House, an ancient inn then on the point of final closure. *(Author)*

The replacement building (II) was a bravura Neo-Baroque exercise in stone on a granite plinth for Smith's Bank by Thomas Isborne of London, who was probably responsible for rebuilding Duffield Hall for Rowland Smith, the bank's proprietor. Inside are bizarre unfluted Corinthian columns, their bases lost to successive rises in floor level by the present proprietors, NatWest. Note the tasteless modern lighting and a corner (right) of Mr Pye's much reviled 'water feature'. *(Author)*

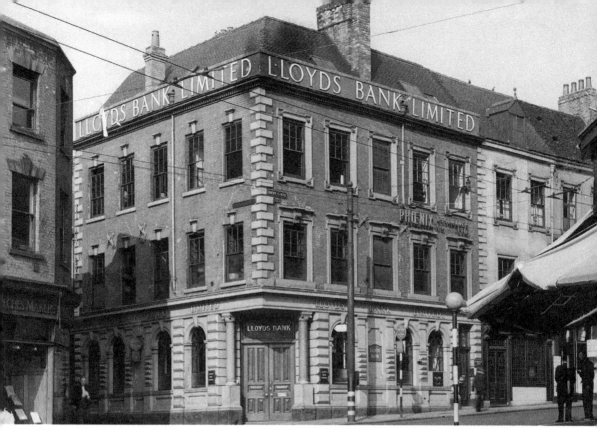

Lloyds Bank, 1947. The late seventeenth-century house on the Iron Gate/Sadler Gate corner (II) has stylistic similarities with Storer's and Franceys' (see top picture on p. 26), as has that next to it, once the George Inn, the façade of which is known to have been put up in 1693 (II). For many years it was the home of the Drewry family, long proprietors of the *Derby Mercury*, but they sold out to William Bemrose in the 1820s, and by the late nineteenth century the ground floor had been rebuilt in rusticated style for Lloyds Bank, as seen here; the unsupported entrance angle with quoins above looks especially gawky. *(Author)*

The Lloyds TSB building, June 2004. In 1953 Lloyds removed the roof, stacks and cornice of this pleasant edifice and gutted most of the interior, a terrible waste and much to the detriment of the street scene. In 1963 Sadler Gate (left) was the first street in Derby to be pedestrianised, at the suggestion of Derby's Civic Society; in 1992 Iron Gate received the same treatment. *(Author)*

Left: Iron Gate photographed by Richard Keene in July 1866. Picturesque in the extreme, Iron Gate's narrowness was considered a great 'hindrance to commerce'. The council, therefore, gradually bought out the leases of all the properties on the east side (right) in order to demolish them and widen the street. The properties are seen already shuttered up in advance of demolition. *(Author)*

Opposite, below: Iron Gate, *c.* 1923. The east side, once cleared, was sold off in freehold plots for new building. The powerful yet subtle Italian palazzo façade of Crompton & Evans's Union Bank of 1880 (II) on the left was by Julius Chatwin of Birmingham. The electric street lighting was installed in 1893. The shops on the right were by a variety of good local architects, H.I. Stevens, F.J. Robinson, Edwin Thompson and others. *(Author)*

Below: In 1992 the whole street was semi-pedestrianised and embellished with Victorian-style street furniture, rather brightly coloured. In the same year, a similar treatment was meted out to the whole of the ancient spinal road through Derby – which long pre-dated the city – all the way to The Spot. Now, in 2004, it is all being redone for some centrally funded scheme mockingly called 'Connecting Derby'. Note a sprinkling of 1950s buildings, put up before the town centre became a conservation area. This postcard dates from 2000. *(Author)*

The view down Iron Gate to Sadler Gate and Rotten Row, as recorded by Keene in May 1855. Until 1784 a wooden beam crossed the street from the light stuccoed building just above the horse. In that year it collapsed, killing a horse; it bore the ornate sign of the George Inn, which became defunct in 1814. The building, right, nearest the camera, is the Talbot Inn (closed and demolished 1877); three bays of the next building were replaced in the 1950s. Everything on the left went in 1866. *(Derby Museum)*

By June 2004 the street had become part of the Derby Promenade – hence the fancy paviours, seats, ersatz gas lamps and planters. The view right down to Burton's in Victoria Street has been opened by the setting back of the buildings on the east side. On the right a couple of 1950s buildings mar the street scene, although at least they are approximately in scale. *(Author)*

A recently discovered Keene photograph of Iron Gate taken from outside the Talbot Inn with Keene's own shop next door. This was where he had his printing business, although he had also taken no. 24 (II), a little further up (out of shot), adding a gallery on the roof to display his photographs. The rebuilding to the right had not been finished; the plot next to the end shop (II), designed by George Henry Sheffield, is still empty, but the street in front of the cathedral had been widened (which occurred in 1873). Note the spire of St Alkmund's in the distance. *(Author)*

By July 1990, 115 years later, Keene's printing shop and the Talbot have long since vanished beneath Crompton & Evans's Union Bank, which was housed in the building next door in the 1870s. Later (until 1997) this was Brigden's, the gentlemen's outfitters and is now Yates's Wine Lodge (II). Unfortunately, the latter firm was allowed to wreck the Queen Anne garden front of the building. *(Author)*

Nos 18–19 Iron Gate, 1872. J. Hives, grocer, and Edwin Cooling, seedsman and florist, occupy a building put up as part of a development that extended some way down St Mary's Gate (right). This was constructed in 1800–2 and financed by Mrs Richardson, the widow of a banker, almost as a modern 'property development', although the grandest house in the St Mary's Gate part was her own residence. The architect was probably John Welch of Derby (1759–1823). Richard Keene (whose gallery can be seen on the building, far left) took the picture on 17 December 1872, with the street bedecked for the visit of HRH the Prince of Wales. *(Derby Museum)*

The same scene in June 2004, and remarkably little has changed. Messrs Clulow, a much-esteemed bookshop that had occupied the site for four generations, closed in 1998, its demise hastened by the coming of Waterstone's. The building (II) was then leased by the cathedral chapter, and later acquired and converted as Derby Cathedral Centre thanks to the inspiration of the Dean, Michael Perham, now Bishop of Gloucester. It was opened by HM the Queen on 14 November 2003. *(Author)*

Queen Street, *c.* 1912. This road was created in the seventeenth century from the southerly portion of medieval King Street and was later widened, in 1926–8. The narrowness of the street can be appreciated, emphasising the soaring bulk of the cathedral tower, completed in 1532 and rising to 207ft to the tops of the vanes that can just be made out on the pinnacles in this view (but no longer extant). The timber-framed inn on the corner of Full Street – the Dolphin (II) – on the left, although a mid-seventeenth-century building, claims a foundation date of 1535. *(Don Gwinnett)*

The effect of broadening the street has been drastic, opening up a vista into Iron Gate. Both streets off – Full Street and Walker Lane (the latter renamed Cathedral Road on widening) – have been widened as well. The timbering on the pub looks different because above it was painted stucco, whereas here it is replacements for the actual timbers which rotted away when the stucco was rather injudiciously removed. The building on the right was originally Sir George Kenning's 1927 car showrooms and is now (inevitably) a café-bar. *(Author)*

Upper St Mary's Gate, *c.* 1895. Whichever way you view the cathedral and its tower it never fails to impress. St Mary's Gate, named after a long-vanished medieval church, was once packed with elegant town houses, the grandest of which, St Mary's Gate House of about 1732, hides behind its Palladian screen and Bakewell gates (see picture on p. 18). Mrs Richardson's house of 1802 (left and see top picture on p. 34) is just visible on the right. *(Author)*

The loss of St Mary's Gate House to make more room for Kenning's in 1938 caused the ugly scar on the left. The house beyond (II), Robotham's, solicitors, is all that remains following the widening of Queen Street, which led to the demolition of the buildings beyond and their replacement by a new office block, set well back. It was during its construction that vestiges of the lost church of St Mary were found. The only change to this scene since 1970, when it was photographed, is the cleaning of the stonework of the tower in 1972. *(The late R.G. Hughes)*

Queen Street, photographed by Keene in May 1855. A very new St Alkmund's Church by Henry Isaac Stevens (1806–73) is seen terminating the view down this ancient thoroughfare. Incidentally, St Alkmund's is neatly hiding the tower of St Mary's, a fact then perceived by Lord Belper as a deliberate anti-Catholic slight, leading him to refuse to subscribe to building the church, although he was resident within its parish. The third house from the left, with Venetian windows, is the later seventeenth-century house of John Flamsteed FRS, and which was re-fronted for John Whitehurst in 1764 by Joseph Pickford. *(Author)*

The same view today is confused by the fact that now St Mary's (II*) terminates the view, and the houses on the left of the previous picture all disappeared in the 1926–8 road-widening. The building with the clock is, however, a re-fronting by Herbert Aslin, for his friend Mr Smith of Smith's clocks, of what was left of the former Whitehurst house after one bay was removed in 1908 and Pickford's façade was sacrificed to the road-widening. The trees mask the canyon through which runs the inner ring road, where once St Alkmund's churchyard stood. *(Author)*

St Michael's Lane, Keene's view northwards from the east end of St Michael's Church, early 1860s. At Sunday communion on 16 August 1856 the chancel collapsed and the church was replaced to a design by Henry Isaac Stevens in the following year, a portion of it being seen in the left foreground. The crumbling seventeenth-century house seen here was a reeking tenement and the arch to the right led into No. 2 Court, which contained two minuscule dwellings. The newness in the two-decade-old spire of St Alkmund's, behind (completed in 1847), is clearly apparent. *(Author)*

The same view today. St Alkmund's was demolished in 1968 and St Michael's was closed in 1972 and converted by Derek Latham into an architects' studio. The long derelict site of the houses opposite was at last built over with the offices of Messrs Edwards Geldard, solicitors, in 1989, but is now occupied by another firm. *(Author)*

St Alkmund's Church, 1860s. St Alkmund's was the site of the earliest church in Derby, sacked by the Norse after 874, and the last medieval church was replaced in 1843–7 by this one. The square in which it stood, linking Bridge Gate with Queen Street, was lined with elegant brick buildings, none later than mid-eighteenth century. The photograph is from C.J. Payne, *Derby Churches Old & New* (1893). *(Author)*

In 1967 this fine square was torn down to make way for the inner ring road. Although the properties were run down – because of a decade of blight inflicted by the coming road – most were listed and some were exceptional. Demolition uncovered seven that incorporated late medieval or sixteenth-century timber framing. The church was dismantled more slowly and the late Dr C.A. Raleigh-Radford excavated the site carefully, revealing much new information about early Derby. The church is seen here in March 1969, after the dig had finished, just prior to being cleared. *(The late R.G. Hughes)*

Nos 53–7 King Street, *c.* 1934. After the First World War this late eighteenth-century house, latterly R.W. Spriggs, grocers, was converted to a motor garage by G.S. Oscroft & Co., Vauxhall concessionaires. Note the tramlines in the road, which had been decommissioned by 1934. This illustration is from the *Bedford Magazine* VI. 7 (11/1935). *(Ashton Antiques, Derby)*

Above: The 1967 move was forced on Pickford Dayton (as it had become) by the building of the inner ring road, which passed under King Street in a deep cutting, framed on the south side by the uncompromising Chapel Street multi-storey car park, producing the scene here. On the right in the distance, marked by trees, may be seen the alignment of the former Great Northern Railway line (closed to all traffic in 1967) which, with a bit of inter-governmental cooperation, could so easily have been made available for the ring road alignment. *(Author)*

The same building in 1953. In 1935 Oscroft's moved to Derwent Street and the premises were taken over by E.H. Pickford & Co., originally from Sheffield and Rootes Group concessionaires after the Second World War. In 1967 the firm moved to Old Chester Road (service) and Duffield Road (sales), being later bought and closed by RTZ, the Old Chester Road premises later revealing one of the most important Roman sites in the county. *(Gerald Redfern)*

Bridge Gate, once the main road to Nottingham, photographed by Richard Keene, *c.* 1855–60. The tower of Pugin's Catholic Church of St Mary dominates the north side of the street. Among the multiplicity of ancient property stands the Nottingham Arms Inn (centre right, with solitary figure standing in front), run until 1791 (as the Sir John Falstaff after a popular China Factory product) by William Billingsley (1758–1828), the celebrated china painter, in succession to his father, who was in charge by 1761. It was later renamed by Billingsley's nephew, William Wheeldon (1789–1847). *(Author)*

Opposite: With the building of the inner ring road in 1967 Bridge Gate was virtually eradicated, leaving but a car-turning circle by St Mary's Presbytery and a footpath alongside some rather poorly designed apartments. In front is an extended Sowter Road, which now dives beneath a very low bridge carrying the new road (left) to reach St Mary's Bridge (II*). This picture from the same viewpoint as that above – the south footpath leading up to St Mary's Bridge shows just how comprehensively this historic streetscape was destroyed. *(Author)*

The Bridge Chapel, woodcut by Llewellyn Jewitt from a drawing made after 1793. There are only six bridge chapels surviving in Britain in any state of repair, and Derby's is one of the most venerable and finest (I). The bridge had replaced a ford called The Causey nearby by 1226, but the chapel was largely rebuilt in the fifteenth century, before being dissolved and, after some vicissitudes, becoming a Presbyterian chapel at the Restoration. Before the end of the eighteenth century the Eaton family had turned it into a hosiery workshop, adding a house for themselves to its west end (II). It became isolated when the medieval bridge was replaced in 1794 by one designed by Thomas Harrison of Chester. *(Author)*

The building of the new bridge (right) led to the rebuilding, in 1793, of the Eatons' house, seen here with its Classical fenestration, by John Finney (1729–1804), architect to the second Improvement Commission. The chapel was revived in the late nineteenth century, restored by Provost Herbert Ham under the careful direction of Percy Currey in 1930 and is now vested in trustees. There are regular services held in its delightful interior. The setting is marred by the building of The Causey inner ring road bridge just feet away to the left. The postcard dates from 4 April 1997. *(The Trustees of the Chapel of St Mary-on-the-Bridge)*

Old St Helen's House, drawn by Sir William Gell from a window of the New Inn, King Street, February 1792. In 1793 the painter Joseph Wright's twenty-one-year lease on the building from William FitzHerbert ended; he it undoubtedly was who adapted the north light windows of the older part of the house (which incorporated parts of the twelfth-century convent and Church of St Helen) to make a studio in 1772. It was demolished in February 1800. This is an 1824 facsimile of the original drawing. *(Private Collection)*

By 1802 the gifted spar turner Richard Brown II (1736–1816) had transferred his works here, complete with Boulton & Watt steam engine to turn lathes from James Fox's works. The marble works (now the only surviving one north of the Alps) – the products of which rivalled those of Matthew Boulton – grew until 1871, when this showroom was added to the proprietor's house, incorporating a former public bath of 1819 at the corner of St Helen's Street. A planned slip road – part of 'Connecting Derby' – will cause the demolition of the complex in 2005, and English Heritage has refused listing applications three times. One really wonders why. *(Author)*

St Helen's House (I) engraving from a drawing by James Stephen Gresley, *c.* 1850. This was built for John Gisborne MP of Yoxall Lodge, Staffordshire, in 1766–7 to designs by Joseph Pickford. It is probably the finest surviving Classical town house outside London. Although Palladian in detail, the design was taken, with the architect's approval, from Robert Adam's Neo Classical Lansdowne House, London. A semicircular courtyard lay behind the screen, and there was Emes parkland to the north. Joseph Wright's friend, the anti-slavery campaigner Thomas Gisborne, sold it to William Strutt FRS who made many improvements of his own devising. *(Author)*

St Helen's House, March 2003. The building is in semi-terminal decline after continuous neglect from 1981 by the County Council and from 1996 by the City Council. Lord Belper sold it to Derby (Grammar) School, later under municipal control. A vast extension was added in 1875–9, to designs by Julian Young, just as road widening led to the loss of the stone screen, with ironwork (as inside) by Benjamin Yates. The obelisk (II) is the Derby School war memorial of 1920 by Sir Reginald Blomfield. The building, for years wasted as a WEA centre, is on the English Heritage 'at risk' register and its future has been mired in controversy since a change of control of the council in 2003 led to its plight becoming public. *(Author)*

2

The Northern Outskirts

North Parade (II), two terraces of eight houses each, was constructed to designs by William Smith of 1819–21 for a building club on part of the grounds of St Helen's House, made available by William Strutt. The terraces were cleaned and refurbished externally in 1991. This view looks south towards the cathedral tower. The hump in the foreground is due to the presence of a former railway bridge over the cutting of the former GNR, filled in 1969. *(Author)*

The Five Lamps, 1901. Here the Kedleston Road (left) diverged from the Duffield Road (foreground and centre), and later Belper Road (*c.* 1893, right) was added to access the former park of St Helen's House, then being developed by Lord Belper. The actual Five Lamps was cast by Weatherhead, Glover & Co. in Duke Street and originally placed at the end of Corn Market in 1837, being moved here in the 1880s. Once electric street lighting arrived it was scrapped. The square house, left, is The Elms (L) of 1801 built for Lancelot Davenport, silk throwster; the roofs showing above the head of the cyclist are those of Woodbines (later Park Grange, by G.H. Sheffield for Sir Clement Bowring, 1878) and the Arts and Crafts house on the right is Derwent House, built in 1898 for Henri Gaspard Pierre LeFanu, physician and surgeon. *(Author)*

Today, on the face of it, there is little difference. The detestable 'Connecting Derby' scheme has led to the reinstatement of a five-light cast-iron standard, but a French reproduction, much inferior in quality, size and design to the Gothic original. Traffic lights (2002) have virtually brought traffic to a halt, and a further phase of the scheme will destroy two elements of a semicircular Edwardian terrace of cottages (out of sight, left), isolate the Seven Stars (II) and St Helen's inns, destroy the marble works and hopelessly compromise the future of St Helen's House – all in order to move the traffic problems from Lodge Lane to Five Lamps. Derwent House is now divided as 'apartments'. *(Author)*

Duffield Road, February 1993. This was created by turnpiking in 1756 and came to be a much sought-after residential area from the Regency period, acquiring during the nineteenth century a stock of fine villas of all periods and styles. This one, Park Field (II), was built in about 1821 and had some Soanian detailing, thanks to prolific amateur architect Alderman Richard Leaper (1759–1838). It was tactfully embellished in the 1880s by Sir John ('Brassy') Smith, incorporating many decorative products from his foundry. In 1921 it became part of a new maternity hospital (Queen Mary's), built in part of the grounds. *(Author)*

Despite being a listed building in a recently designated conservation area, approval was given for Park Field to be destroyed in 1993. A much-favoured local developer built Queen Mary's Court in its place. Amusingly, at least two councillors immediately bought homes in the development. Yet Park Field, with the hospital removed, could have been reconverted into one or more delightful residences and still left room for a more sympathetic development. *(Author)*

Darley Abbey, 1971. From the top of Duffield Road one descends into Darley Abbey, an almost perfectly preserved, largely Regency mill village. Until 1538 it was the county's largest monastery, but on the Dissolution it was converted into a country house. This building (II*), seen here in a state of collapse after over a century divided as artisans' cottages, is thought to be the only substantial surviving abbey building, albeit of unknown purpose. *(Don Farnsworth)*

Darley Abbey, July 2003. Derby architect Richard Wood finally managed to acquire the building, convince the locals that they wanted a pub after 150 years without one (the natives wanted one, the incomers didn't!) and get the necessary permissions sorted out. In the end he managed to convert the building with some panache into the Abbey Inn. It opened on 5 October 1979 and has proved a great success. *(Author)*

Darley Abbey. It is unclear when Richard Keene took this photograph, but it was not the only one he took of virtually the same scene, which underwent little change throughout the nineteenth century. It shows Darley House, built in about 1794 for Thomas Evans, banker and Darley cotton-mill entrepreneur, probably to the amateur designs of his son-in-law William Strutt, who designed all his family's houses. The church (II) is by Henry Moses Wood, 1818 (for the Evans family), and at the extreme right can be seen a portion of the family's mills, driven by the fall of water from the weir. *(Author)*

Today the mills are divided up as small industrial and business units. Darley House has gone (demolished 1934), its park, denuded of trees, now covered in postwar housing. Keene's view, though, thanks to a prohibition on access to the island on which he stood, is virtually impossible to replicate. *(Author)*

Darley House and Darley Abbey Mills depicted on this specially com-missioned Bloor Derby plate. Banker Thomas Evans (1723–1814) acquired the site through having been appointed commissioner in bankruptcy for John and Christopher Heath (also bankers). Spurred on by his familial ties with the entrepre-neurial Strutt family, Evans built a cotton mill here between 1781 and 1783, in which latter year the enterprise burnt down and had to be restarted. The mills were called Boar's Head Mills after the crest granted to the Evans family in 1815 and were in their heyday at exactly that date. *(Mellors & Kirk)*

Almost the same scene, but looking north rather than north-west, November 1983. The mills (I, II*, II) have largely survived, and since 2002 have been included in the Derwent Valley World Heritage Site. Indeed, they are the most original and best preserved of all the mills in the WHS. The low portion, left, has for a long time been a very good restaurant. *(Author)*

The junction of Kedleston Road with Penny Long Lane on the then borough boundary, *c.* 1912. The tram has stopped preparatory to changing track for the return journey to Derby. The attractive house was built as Cloverley by Derby architect Arthur Eaton (1857–1924) in 1892–3 for chemist W.B. Sherwin, but by 1908 it had become a private nursing home. In 1952 it was converted into a hotel – the name subtly changed to Clovelly – and such it remained until 1994. At this point part of it was converted into a pub named after Sir Garfield Sobers by its owner Roger Pearman, a former Middlesex player and once chief executive of Derbyshire CCC. *(Don Gwinnett)*

The same view, June 2004. The corner on which the Clovelly Hotel stood was complicated in 1938 by the completion from here to Duffield Road of the Derby ring road as Broadway, which isolated Penny Long Lane. This, though, brought the potential trade that had prompted its opening in 1952, but in the 1970s, after years of work, the A38 road scheme was completed, once more turning this enclave into a quiet piece of suburbia, with the trunk-road traffic roaring along in a cutting. In 1992 the 1960s technical college became a university and the area was changed forever. Finally, the allure of a rocketing housing market led to the completely unnecessary demolition of the hotel (it would have converted beautifully) and its replacement by banal flats. *(Author)*

West Parkfields, 1999. An unexceptional but lavishly fitted villa, it was built in about 1873 for George Dean of Dean & Bowcock, elastic web manufacturers of Stockbrook Street (hence also nearby Dean Street), and designed by Giles & Brookhouse of Derby. It was originally called Park Villa, but by 1878 had been renamed. In about 1894 it was sold to E.T. (later Sir Edwin) Ann (1852–1913), who was knighted as Mayor of Derby when King Edward VII made a semi-state visit in 1906; he was founder and proprietor of the Midland Drapery, St Peter's Street (closed 1971). *(Sheila Tarling)*

The house and its extensive grounds passed in 1913 to the younger son, William Eastland Ann JP, after whose death in December 1934 the house appears to have been sold for conversion as the Queen Victoria Memorial Home of Rest, moved from Douglas House, 228 Osmaston Road. More recently it was the Wheeldon Manor (named after the Victorian owner of neighbouring Parkfields House) residential home. In 2000 it was sold, and was demolished a year later in order to build this meretricious apartment block, also optimistically called Wheeldon Manor – Ann Manor might have been more appropriate. *(Author)*

3

Derwent's Edge

Derby's delightful chapel of St Mary-on-the-Bridge (I), with its house behind and the 1794 St Mary's Bridge (II*) to the right, designed by Thomas Harrison of Chester, seen here in 1954. Behind (left) is the slim spire of H.I. Stevens's Church of St Alkmund (built 1843–6, demolished 1968) and (right) the nave roof and pinnacles of Pugin's St Mary (II*) (1838–44). *(Author)*

Opposite: Silk Mill gates, photographed by Keene before 1860. Robert Bakewell made these gates (I) in about 1718, crowning the overthrow with the two crossed tilting spears that the Lombes bore for a crest. This photograph shows that some restoration work was needed, repoussé work having been lost from each end of the overthrow and elsewhere, with some smaller bars missing too. It was not until the building of the Municipal Electricity Power Station adjacent that they were sent to Edwin Haslam (1843–1913) for restoration. Haslam, brother of Mayor Sir Alfred Haslam, followed his father in reviving wrought-iron gate-making, bringing to it an Arts and Crafts flair. Note the painted notice on the right pier:

NOTICE
NO PERSON IS
ALLOWED TO NET
OR ANGLE IN THE
WATERS ADJOINING
THESE MILLS

(Author)

The Silk Mill gates, 1982. For much of the twentieth century the gates stood beside the library in The Wardwick. Each May Day a wreath was laid upon them to commemorate the 1833 silk strike, although its effects were hardly felt at the Silk Mill proper, the event a slightly cathartic and purely symbolic gesture on the part of those who hold such things dear. In 1980 the gates were taken down and again restored, being transferred back to the Silk Mill (where the wreath ceremony is still most solemnly performed) and re-erected in April 1981. *(Author)*

Derby Silk Mill, photographed by Keene not long before the water wheel was removed, *c.* 1855. The Silk Mill (II) was completed for Sir Thomas and John Lombe in 1718, and the Derby engineer George Sorocold provided the design, the mill race and the (then) unprecedentedly large water wheel which drove all the 'Italian Machines'. Defoe tells us that Sorocold fell into the mill race while over-enthusiastically demonstrating the ingenuity of his design. The buildings beyond are Brown's former spar workshop, John Lombe's house and (left) William Brown's corn mill. *(Author)*

Repeating the previous view has been impossible since the power station expanded on to the site of the mill race in the 1920s, forcing the camera back on to the earlier part of the power station site, now cleared as Cathedral Green. The mill was acquired on lease by Derby Borough Council and opened in 1974 as the Industrial Museum, hence the small locomotives on display outside in this June 1980 photograph. Final traces of the mill race outfall were removed during operations to 'beautify' the river frontage in 1991. *(Author)*

Derby Silk Mill, photographed by Keene, *c*. 1865. This atmospheric image of a glassy calm Derwent was taken from the point where the Darley extension of the Derby Canal once debouched into the river by J. & G. Haywood's Phoenix Foundry. The mill was gutted by fire in 1821, and in rebuilding acquired its distinctive arcaded tower (the twin of one provided by William Strutt's friend Kirk Boott on one of his mills at Lowell, Massachusetts, USA) and hipped roof. The chimney marks the impending replacement of waterpower by steam. Pickford's weir remains, but not apparently doing much! *(Author)*

The photographer's position in the previous view is now occupied by the Causey bridge, carrying the 1968 inner ring road over the Derwent. The mill itself is now lower, having again been gutted by fire in 1910 and rebuilt with only three storeys. At that time Alderman Unwin Sowter's bakery, corn and maltings firm (successors of William Brown's) also burnt out and they added a large mill to the northern end. The weir has long gone, and a distinct greening of the riverbank has taken place. Derby City Council bought the freehold of the Silk Mill from the nationalised electricity undertaking when the lease ran out, ensuring the future of the museum. *(Author)*

The riverbank from Exeter Bridge. This calotype photograph is marked on the mount 'W. Stretch/1855' which is enigmatic, W. Stretch not being a name recorded in Derby at that time, especially as a photographer. It is a little coarse for a Keene, but still could be by him or perhaps Canon Edward Abney, his mentor, if one assumes that the (contemporary) inscription refers to the subject: the westerly stretch of the Derwent. Once again, the scene is dominated by the Silk Mill, the separate Doubling Shop (which collapsed in September 1890 and was demolished) and the tall atmospheric engine-house between, added in the 1730s to heat the building to obviate the snapping of the silk filaments in cold weather. The two churches are St Alkmund's and St Mary's, with the former town-house gardens of Full Street being rapidly encroached upon by industry, such as the tall flour mill (left). *(Derby Museum)*

Opposite, above: Virtually the same scene, also from Exeter Bridge, 1950. The Silk Mill, reduced by the 1910 fire, is here dominated by the hideously utilitarian and recently nationalised Municipal Electricity Supply Station, built from 1893 in ever uglier stages. Only Derby could allow such a behemoth to be plonked next to one of the finest Baroque parish churches in England! On the left is the highly urbane river front of the 1934 magistrates' courts (II) by C.H. Aslin CBE, as borough architect, part of his grand Central Improvement Plan; the courts closed in 2003. He rightly saw that the bravura frontages of new buildings should present themselves to the river, a lesson since, unfortunately, forgotten. *(Private Collection)*

Opposite, below: The view north up the Derwent to the Silk Mill from the terrace of the magistrates' courts on a snowy morning in 1988. The power station is gone (demolished 1971) giving James Gibbs's All Saints' room to breathe, but this has opened up the prospect of the surviving transformer station, hidden behind a great blank brick wall next to the Silk Mill. Within two years the former industrial buildings of the east bank of the river – which had a sort of mature charm – were replaced by banal computer-designed office blocks presenting their most unattractive side to the river. In the distance is one of Derby's three tower blocks, the low-lying Rivermead House, Bath Street (T. East, 1963). *(Author)*

Full Street, photographed by Keene in the 1850s. Within two decades the gabled mansion on the right had had its central portion built up by a storey. This house had been built in the later seventeenth century but by 1780 was the home of the Revd Henry Peach of Kirk Langley (1754–1833), a friend of all the great and good and a lavish entertainer. Beyond can just be discerned the side of the end gable of Joseph Pickford's Devonshire Hospital (1777) with Burdett's House (Gothic, also Pickford) and the Corporation Baths (H.I. Stevens, 1852) lying back, out of sight, between them. *(Derby Museum)*

In 1893 the almshouses Pickford endowed behind such an elegant Palladian screen were demolished to make way for the first phase of the corporation's electricity power station. Their demise was followed in 1904 by that of the Classical stone-fronted baths, replaced by a fine building away in Reginald Street. John Ward and Alexander MacPherson then designed the main façade of the power station, seen here shortly before its destruction in 1971, with the brand new eastern extension of the cathedral (designed by Sebastian Comper) just visible, left. *(Don Farnsworth)*

The most enlightened thing any recent Derby council ever did was to grass over the site of the power station and restrain themselves from building on it. This had the effect of opening up the east end of the church to the river, framed by decent buildings. Unfortunately, the entirely unaccountable urban regeneration company, Derby CityScape, following slavishly an idea thought up by consultants BDP, want to encourage the building of 'prestige apartments' down either side of the green, a potential disaster if ever there was one. For the present the area is now embellished only by Anthony Stones's fine equestrian bronze of HRH Prince Charles Edward, paid for by Lionel Pickering, and rather reluctantly accepted by the council to mark the 250th anniversary of the 'Forty Five'. *(Author)*

Derby Council House. The centrepiece of the 1931 Central Improvement Plan was the Derby Council House (L), only a shell when the Second World War broke out, and immediately requisitioned. It was later completed without much of the intended detail, which included a stone pylon above its grand pedimented entrance, and without anything but utility furniture within, giving the mayor's reception suite a spartan air. For all that it is still a tour de force of a building. The river arch marks the outfall of the culverted Markeaton Brook, the higher one a link to a separate intended council chamber. This is one of C.H. Aslin's perspectives, and compares very well with the building from the same angle in 1975. *(Author, by permission of His Worship the Mayor of Derby)*

The same scene in 1975, and barely changed since. Aslin designed a sweeping serpentine stepped riverbank to contrast with the four-square building and lead the eye to his predecessor's Exeter Bridge (1929–31). It also forms part of the riverside gardens laid out as a memorial to the fallen of the First World War, but later simplified and now to be destroyed by a gimcrack new scheme to be called Riverlights, originally intended as shops and offices but now to be flats and bars. The latest insult is that the incoming council found that the Council House is riddled with asbestos, as a result of which routine maintenance had long since been curtailed. It is to be evacuated as soon as a replacement can be found. On the positive side, it would make an excellent five-star hotel with an incomparable position, something that the city has long needed. *(Author)*

The Long Bridge, 1947. When Benjamin Outram completed the Derby canal, which linked the Trent & Mersey at Swarkestone with the Erewash canal via Derby in 1796, the crossing of the Derwent was made by raising Pickford's weir and constructing another below the line of the canal. This maintained the Derwent at the correct level for navigation. He also provided a timber causeway to carry the towpath across from Cockpit Hill Wharf to White Bear Lock. It is seen here from the Council House embankment, with part of the new cattle market behind (H.I. Stevens and George Thompson, 1861). *(The late A. Wilson)*

Today the scene is barely recognisable with the Long Bridge demolished after the canal's demise in 1964. The coming of the inner ring road at this point, in 1971, caused the destruction and relocation of the new cattle market and the swamping of this stretch of the Derwent with the huge concrete Holmes Bridge, mercifully now embowered by trees after thirty-three years; only the tall floodlights and the end of a sign gantry give away the fact that there is a massive system of dual carriageways lurking behind the boscage! *(Author)*

Exeter Bridge, photographed by Keene in about 1855. The foundry erected on the future site of the Council House had yet to be built when this was taken. The site is still marked by the bosky river frontage of the late medieval timber-framed town house called The Old Mayor's Parlour (demolished 1948). The camera is at the point where the Long Bridge met the west bank of the Derwent, and shows the elegant and then nearly new second Exeter Bridge, designed by James Trubshaw of Great Heywood, Staffordshire (1777–1853), replaced in 1931. *(Author)*

A view taken from a point on Holmes Bridge as near as one can get to that above, 2000. The 1931 bridge can be seen, still with trees by its east abutments, with Aslin's Exeter House Flats of 1931–2 in the centre, almost masking the enjoyable Regency pub the Exeter Arms (L) on the right, established here on what used to be called Canary Island in 1816 and twice refused a listing by English Heritage. Once the canal was gone the opportunity was taken to decommission the upper weir and make a new, very large one on the site of the Long Bridge – a mistake really, for it prevents some entrepreneur from offering boating on the river. The large, ugly building to the left is the Assembly Rooms multi-storey car park, towering over Aslin's magistrates' courts. *(Author)*

Opposite, above: This painting is called *The Morledge, Derby, in Fair Time, 1882* by gentleman amateur the Revd Charles Thomas Moore of Appleby Parva (died 1922). Although not technically of the first rank, it is a very jolly and largely accurate account of the Morledge from Cockpit Hill. In the left distance, below the cupola of the Guildhall, are Tower Buildings, still standing; the centre is dominated by the shot tower, built by Cox Bros, lead merchants, in 1809 with All Saints' tower behind, St Alkmund's and St Mary's receding into the right distance. To the right is Melbourne-born Alderman Robert Pegg's colour works. *(Derby Museum, Goodey Collection No. 352)*

Opposite, below: Easter Fair, Derby, April 1913. Amazingly, the skyline has changed little: the shot tower and the colour works (right) both lasted until clearance for the Central Improvement Plan in 1931, although the fairs were relegated to Alvaston then and, after 1945, to Bass's recreation ground on The Holmes. The bell turret of the Silk Mill can just be seen in a gap, half right. And, what a delight to get one's hands on half the things on those stalls. *(Derby Museum)*

In 1972 Cockpit Hill was cleared for the erection of the Eagle Centre Market (see p. 69), itself of necessity rebuilt in 1991. Thus one has to stand inside the new building to approximate the view of 1882 and 1913 as here (in a photograph taken in February 1995). The only point of reference is the cathedral tower, contrasting with the vast bulk of the Assembly Rooms cutting a horizontal swathe through the middle distance. Tower Buildings are left of the white van, Morledge has been dualled (1932) and a corner of the Council House can be discerned far right. *(Author)*

Derby Bus Station, *c.* 1935. In place of the colour works of Alderman Pegg, Herbert Aslin built a state-of-the-art bus station which, because of the constrictions of the site, had to be laid out on a parabolic plan. The internal arrangement was derived from railway practice and was said to have been based on an example in the New World. The style was unashamedly *Moderne*, the terminal building being a drum externally decorated with reliefs, with a marble-sheathed circulating hall, café, enquiry office, etc., between symmetrical wings containing retail units in canted bays. It has a good capacity and works well from an operational point of view. Note the vast fleet of idle buses parked behind, right. *(Author)*

Derby Bus Station, 2002. Today the place has a worn, tawdry look, having been blighted by Messrs MetroHolst's dreadful Riverlights scheme, which will replace this felicitously designed complex with a smaller capacity one beneath one of the elements of the new scheme. An imaginative refurbishment with better facilities for travellers would have created a showpiece, but the usual English Heritage refusal to list – because the canopies had been cut back to accommodate longer vehicles and the control tower had gone – cleared the way for eventual demolition. *(Author)*

Cockpit Hill, photographed by Keene's son, Charles Barrow Keene, October 1931. The Canal Tavern of 1800 is seen on the right. Cockpit Hill appears on John Speed's map of 1610 with a cockpit on top. It was surrounded by strangely shaped boundaries, and may have had some connection with the twelfth-century adulterine castle believed to have been built hereabouts by the Earl of Chester during the Anarchy. *(Derby Museum)*

Cockpit Hill area, 1973. From 1969 to 1972 all this was swept away to build what turned out to be quite one of Britain's worst early shopping centres, the Eagle Centre. Note the new, brutalist Castle and Falcon Inn (replacing a nice building of 1819) and 1960s developments in East Street behind. The area has recently undergone its second major rebuild, but has now changed hands and an Australian company, Westfield, wisely plan to raze it completely and replace it with something more 'up-to-date and humane'. *(Raymonds)*

Cockpit Hill area, May 2004. The 1991 rebuilding of the Eagle Centre Market resulted in a much more coherent, user-friendly building, with the added advantage that it masks the ugly Castle and Falcon. Although the corner building, right, remains from the 1960s, the one behind the pub has been replaced by a quite admirable building in a good unpretentious post-Classical style. The oversized advertising rotunda, supplied by the ubiquitous M. Decaux (why do all council officials seem to fall over themselves to choose this French manufacturer of tacky street furniture?), does little for the scene. *(Author)*

A Derby teacup, decorated with a view of the Derby China Factory, of about 1800. Derby's Nottingham Road has never been a showpiece, but it was the location, for almost a century, for the Derby China Factory, founded in about 1750. No authentic view of the works survives save a drawing done from memory by Moses Webster almost forty years after its demise, another speculative view and some enigmatic architects' drawings in the local collection, one being of a weighbridge house by Joseph Pickford. There was intense interest, then, when this cup surfaced in a sale in Derby in 1999. *(Neales)*

Approximately the same scene today reveals a realigned Nottingham Road dominated by its elevated concrete successor – nameless, just the A52 – built in 1969, reducing it to a dead end serving the shops and houses on the Liversage Trust Estate beyond. Past the single surviving nineteenth-century cottage seen here, two mid-eighteenth-century ones (L) can be found further round. One is the former Punch Bowl Tavern of 1758, which was closed in 1908 through temperance movement pressure and is now a private house. To the left is the City Technology College, the Landau Forte College of 1993 with Phoenix Street in the foreground, diving beneath the inner ring road. *(Author)*

4

Corn Market & the Southern Approaches

A parade in Corn Market, *c.* 1922. No information is known about this photograph,
except that it is clearly before the Iron Gate/Market Place corner was rebuilt for Barlow,
Taylor & Co. in 1924. It is also high summer, for the light is evening light and the time
6.55 p.m. The Salvation Army are much in evidence, along with a determined-looking
bunch of tinies, suggesting a Sunday. The crowds are
particularly dense. What can be going on? *(M. Allseybrook Esq.)*

Corn Market, *c.* 1936. The width of Corn Market derives from its role from medieval times to 1861 as a street where grains were traded from basins supported on posts ('stoups'). Left of centre is Devonshire House (II), a 1755 re-fronting for the Duke of Devonshire, and beyond it Pickford's former Tiger Inn of 1764 (II). The white building in the centre is the Admiral Rodney Inn, rebuilt as the 'New Rodney Wine & Spirit Establishment' for Loughborough wine merchant Julius Mott to the designs of Henry Goddard of Leicester in 1836. The half-timbered building next door was an 1890s rebuilding of the former Old Angel Inn, property of the College of All Saints in 1536. *(Author)*

Corn Market, 1979. The greatest disaster to hit Corn Market was on the night of 31 December 1968, when the contractors of Messrs Littlewood's removed a few stones from the parapet of Devonshire House. The following morning legislation came into effect requiring the owners of listed buildings to seek permission to alter or demolish instead of merely notifying. Thus were lost five out of nine bays of Devonshire House, the Rodney, the Old Angel and two other buildings to a horrifically ugly concrete store, just visible on the right. *(Author)*

Corn Market, 2000. Poetic justice caught up with Littlewood's, however, and their store closed in the 1990s to be replaced by an extension of Marks & Spencer. This view shows the 1992 Derby Promenade before it was all ripped up again at the caprice of a council of a different persuasion to that which laid it out, aided by a colossal government grant. This scheme, part of the notorious 'Connecting Derby', led to the removal of the triple steel arch (just visible right), a work of art of 1992 intended to celebrate Derby's tradition of wrought-iron-making – perhaps no loss. *(Author)*

Lower St Peter's Street. This Keene view of the east side of the street north of East Street has been published before, but shows it virtually unchanged since the eighteenth century with the exception of George & George's shop (formerly Joseph Strutt's Regency town house) in the distance. Edward Johnson, a prolific clockmaker, was established in 1851 and moved in 1875; careful analysis of his neighbours in the directories establishes the date of this photograph to be between 1865 and 1870. *(Author)*

Below: Lower St Peter's Street, 1999. From 1882 these shops began to be replaced by the ever-expanding Midland Drapery of Alderman E.T. Ann; lower down they were replaced piecemeal from the later nineteenth century. George & George gave way to the HSBC building (II) by J.S. Story 1880–2 (far left); the Midland Drapery was closed and swept away in 1971 in favour of the dreary and under-scale Audley Centre (far right); and in 1936 the properties in between were replaced by an Empire-style branch of Marks & Spencer (L) in Portland stone, designed in the firm's then 'house style' by Robert Lutyens, son of the famous Sir Edwin. *(Author)*

Upper St Peter's Street looking north from just above St Peter's, *c.* 1898. The then still-expanding Midland Drapery can be seen right of centre, marked by the giant rooftop magnet sign that was supposed to draw the people in. The shop next to it (on the East Street corner) and the pedimented one beside it went in 1910 to make way for Boots' store; those nearer to the camera followed in 1913 to make way for the colossal Whitehall Electric Theatre – very Albert Speer, but by T.H. Thorpe in white glazed facings – which opened in 1914. *(Don Gwinnett)*

As before, the distance is occupied by Jefferson's (II; now H. Samuel) of 1848 on the Albert Street Corn Market corner, but where the majestic Midland Drapery stood there is only the tawdry Audley Centre. Miraculously, everything on the west side of the street has so far survived – although recent experience has shown that unlisted buildings in Derby's conservation areas are extremely vulnerable. The street is now fully pedestrianised. *(Author)*

St Peter's Church, 1860s. St Peter's Street did not need widening until one reached the church. G. Gordon Place of Nottingham rebuilt the church in 1851–3 (adding a big new vicarage away up the Burton Road), but the widening and replacement churchyard wall were done in 1858–9 along with a restoration of the chancel by Derby architect John Price (1795–1859); as the rotunda building just beyond the church (see left of centre in both photos on p. 74) was not erected until 1879, the photograph from which this heliotype was taken must have been between 1859 and 1878, but probably in the 1860s, for the new shops (right) look brand new. *(Author)*

Below: St Peter's Church, 1992. The church underwent further rebuildings too. While Price was reworking the chancel, the remainder was receiving a 'sensitive restoration' by George Edmund Street (which doesn't say much for the durability of Place's work!). Indeed, Price's work was what survives, nearest the camera, for the whole of the rest of the church was taken right down and rebuilt by the little known John Hawley Lloyd of Birmingham in 1897–8 – note how the tower has changed. It was then that the old clock (allegedly by Robert Bakewell) was replaced by one made by Smith of Derby, along with a new dial. *(Author)*

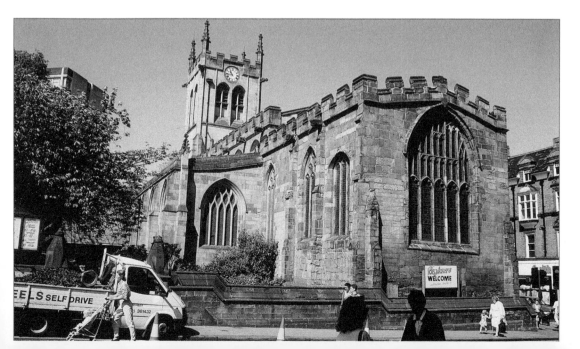

An ink drawing of St Peter's churchyard, 1840s. Gordon Place's restoration of St Peter's Church (B) took place just a few months before Keene took his first photographs, so this drawing is the only record of the tower as it was previously, with its off-centre louvered lancets with their almost Saxon stone framing. In front is Derby (Grammar) School, still then in use, founded by charter in 1555, although the building (II*) would appear to date from some fifty years later. The cottages bounding the north side of the churchyard (then not a thoroughfare) belonged to the Liversage charity. *(Author)*

St Peter's churchyard, May 1992. Today the scene is not radically different. The old grammar school is still there, with the church behind, albeit with Mr Lloyd's tower in succession to Place's effort (see top picture on p. 75). In about 1973 Derek Montague added the modernist portico to the school when it became Raymond's studios; it has now become Derby's (commercial) Heritage Centre – essentially a characterful café with locally focused bookshop and a rota of temporary displays. Yet just off to the right is a huge concrete office block on Gower Street. How long this small sward will remain undeveloped it is impossible to say. *(Author)*

A postcard view of St Peter's Street north from the junction with Babington Lane, 1905. The building on the corner occupies the site of the early Tudor gatehouse of Babington Hall, where Mary, Queen of Scots stayed on 13 January 1585. The gatehouse was demolished in about 1811 and the structure seen here was erected as a speculation by builder Joseph Gascoyne (1784–1865) in 1852–3. Babington Lane was created by the Improvement Commission in 1789. *(Don Gwinnett)*

The same view, May 2004. The Derby Promenade eliminated traffic from St Peter's Street, but buses still needed to get from Babington Lane to The Spot, hence the reconfiguration of the road. Mr Gascoyne's building has lost its chimneys and balustrading but, worse still, that next door was replaced in the early 1960s with this truly dire glass and concrete white-painted building constructed for a building society. On the east side nearly everything has been replaced (mainly in the 1970s) and it is notable that the new build is, without exception, low and mean, wrecking the street scene. *(Author)*

The Spot is a name unknown before 1741 for the junction of London Road (turnpiked in the 1750s) and Osmaston Road; its origin is utterly obscure. Maltster Abraham Ward may have first coined this name for his own premises: was the four-bay three-storey curved building situated on the inside of the junction the original Spot? This pre-1904 lithographic postcard shows the streetscape barely changed since Ward's day, bar the large shop on the far right, built in 1897–8. *(Author)*

On 28 June 1906 a statue of Queen Victoria by Charles Bell Birch was unveiled at The Spot by her son Edward VII en route to the Royal Show at Osmaston Park. In 1911 the road was widened by demolition of Ward's building and those immediately behind it on either side. In typical Derby fashion, the site then lay derelict behind hoardings until the 1930s. *(Author)*

The quality may be poor but this planning department photograph of The Spot in the rush hour is extraordinary for its endless vistas of trolley buses jammed tight along Osmaston Road, 12 April 1962. The public toilets were installed in 1928, but poor Queen Victoria was banished to the grounds of the DRI as she was too heavy for the newly created labyrinth beneath! Meanwhile, Victoria's ownership passed with the hospital from the municipality to the NHS, who meanly refused to return her to Victoria Street in 1993. *(Author)*

The view today is largely vehicle-free thanks to the council's 1991 Derby Promenade. Traffic is permitted to pass round the inside of the angle, and disabled parking is allowed down to Babington Lane. The Promenade was terminated with a new clock-tower feature designed by the city's architects in a debased *Moderne* style to echo that of the corner building by Sir Frederick Bennett & Partners, 1934. Needless to say, it is universally known as the 'gun emplacement'. *(Author)*

The Spot from London Road, photographed by Keene on the occasion of a visit from HRH Edward, Prince of Wales, 15 July 1881. The street was decorated with a floral arch paid for out of the deep pockets of Alderman Sir Abraham Woodiwiss (1828–84), then mayor for the second successive time – doubtless re-elected in the knowledge that he would be generous! Through the right arch is Babington House (formerly Sitwell Hall), built by the Borough's first ever mayor, Henry Mellor, in 1626. By this date its forecourt had been infilled with shops. *(Derek Jewell)*

It is a measure of the drastic manner in which the angle on the left was cut back in 1911 that Babington Buildings – erected in 1897–8 to designs of Methodist chapel architect John Wills for Councillor Fletcher of the Public Benefit Boot & Shoe Company and now Waterstone's – stand to the far right of this scene. The front of the curved building in the photograph at the top of the page (left) came to where the third taxi from the right is standing, next to the 'gun emplacement' marking the start of the Derby Promenade. The vast office block behind was built on Babington Lane in the 1970s. *(Author)*

London Road viewed from the corner of Bradshaw Street (left) after the demolition of the graceful Swedenborgian chapel of 1819 for the large block of shops (centre) in 1902 and before electrification of the tramways in July 1904. The pedimented building is H.I. Stevens's Congregational chapel of 1846 on the corner of Traffic Street. *(Don Gwinnett)*

In 1962–3 Bradshaw Street was dualled and joined by a huge roundabout to Traffic Street, already widened and realigned in 1935 and now also dualled, necessitating the removal of Stevens's chapel, adapted by T.H. Thorpe as the Coliseum (*sic*) cinema in 1935. The demise, in 1961, of Boden's Silk Mill, behind, has paved the way for the truly ghastly Main Centre (itself due for demolition in 2005), causing the demolition of the rest of the buildings visible above. A new pub, however, was built in 1982 (behind the bus, centre) and duly named the Coliseum, but was not actually on the chapel's site. It was hilariously renamed Baroque in 2000 but is also due to be demolished in 2005. *(Author)*

Derby station, photographed by Thomas Scotton, *c.* 1888. In 1862 the railway company took over the hotel, while the station was rebuilt in 1871 to designs of accomplished MR architect John Holloway Sanders (1826–84) – the son of the general manager Joseph Sanders (who says nepotism is a bad thing?). He added a portecochère and raised Thompson's façade by one storey in the central section, producing a handsome result. *(Derby Museum)*

Engraving of Derby station, *c.* 1843. The station was built in 1839 for the three companies, which in 1844 amalgamated to form the Midland Railway, and was designed by the North Midland Railway's architect Francis Thompson (1808–95). All three shared one enormously long platform. On the right here is Thompson's Midland Hotel (II), which was built by London contractor Thomas Jackson on his own initiative and opened on 1 June 1841. *(Author)*

Below: Derby station, 1905. In 1892–3, the station was again rebuilt, by Sanders' successor Charles Trubshaw (1841–1917), and thus it remained with Thompson's largely unaltered and imposing original façade behind. However, in 1983 British Rail announced that they were going to demolish the entire thing as it was 'inconvenient and outmoded'. Derby Civic Society, SAVE Britain's Heritage and others fought passionately for its listing and retention, but to no avail and it was largely demolished in 1985. *(Author)*

The station was replaced by what Dr Gavin Stamp called a 'hi-tech shack' designed by BR architect Bernard Kaukas, who had earlier tried to bring the Civic Society's architectural adviser before a RIBA disciplinary tribunal, so heated was the debate about the station's future! All this six months after the city council had declared the locality a Conservation Area, before cravenly caving in to BR bullying. *(Author)*

A sylvan view north up Swarkestone Road, Chellaston, painted by Frank Gresley (1855–1936), *c.* 1880. Gresley lived in the village for most of his life after his marriage to the daughter of a Derby pub landlord in 1875. The building on the left is the Rose & Crown Inn, certainly a going concern in 1753 and still flourishing today. The farmhouse, right of centre, was replaced by a Derby Co-operative Society shop in 1915, erected at a cost of £1,400. *(Mellors & Kirk)*

The Rose & Crown, 2004. The pub was totally rebuilt in the decades following the Second World War, only its thatched extension surviving intact, but even that was re-roofed in tile. The Co-op was replaced – quite why is unclear – by a new Co-op supermarket, which retained the half-timbered theme but sported a ridiculous little clock turret on the angle. What was once a quiet rural village has been transformed, since incorporation into the City in 1968, into a still-expanding residential suburb, with very few original buildings surviving and absolutely none of the ambience that still lingers in some of the older suburbs. *(Author)*

Rolls-Royce Works, 1913. The company moved to Derby from Manchester in 1907, having acquired a substantial chunk of the former Osmaston Hall estate on the west side of Osmaston Road at a very reasonable price. The works were opened in 1908, and the 380ft long 'commercial block' – designed personally by Sir Henry Royce and built by Andrew Handyside & Co. of Duke Street – was completed in the autumn of 1912. Royce designed the sills of the three- and four-light mullioned windows awkwardly high, so that people working in the offices could not see out from their desks and be distracted from their work! The Mess House in the foreground is dated 1910. *(Author)*

In 1937–8 the company, frequently host to parties of high-ranking dignitaries, often from abroad, put in a bravura Art-Deco centrepiece in Portland stone. The interior was lavishly decorated with marble and, thereafter, became universally known as the Marble Hall. The old 'centre' of the building (at bay sixteen out of thirty-six) had been a cramped, double staircase but thereafter the building had much more *gravitas*. At the same time the entire block was widened at the rear. Unfortunately, Rolls-Royce are planning to vacate the site soon, and will, no doubt, be looking to maximise their profit on it, putting this historically important but unlisted complex at dire risk. *(Peter Billson)*

The Arboretum, 1907. John Claudius Loudon (1783–1843) laid out this 11-acre public park (II) for the philanthropical cotton manufacturer Joseph Strutt in 1840. Most of the buildings are by Edward Buckton Lamb, but the Orangery, left of centre, with the entrance lodge on its other side, dates from 1853 and is the work of Henry Duesbury (died 1872). The houses in the square beyond were by Charles Humphreys, 1865–7. The park itself was scattered with pieces of sculpture from Strutt's own garden, including the terracotta copy of the Florentine Boar by William John Coffee (1773–1846), right. *(Author)*

The Arboretum, June 2004. Time, industrial pollution and the Second World War 'dig for victory' campaign did nothing for Loudon's design, added to which, many of the sculptures were either stolen or melted down for scrap in the war. The boar itself was smashed by shrapnel from the Victorian bandstand, which received a direct hit from a bomb. The Derbyshire Historic Buildings Trust restored the Orangery as photographers' studios in 1991, and a lottery grant has been obtained to restore the rest. Unfortunately, the restoration of the boar by a replica has been hit by rampant political correctness, for a so-called focus group thought it *might* offend the Muslim population in the vicinity. *(Author)*

Sir Henry Royce (1863–1933) brooding over the decay of this important listed park and his imminent removal, 1971. The Arboretum was originally thought to be the ideal spot for this statue, sculpted by Derwent Wood RA in 1921 (II) in his subject's lifetime – an extremely rare honour. *(Author)*

Above: Statue of Sir Henry Royce, outside the Council House, *c.* 1972. After leaving the Arboretum, room was made for him by Herbert Aslin in his Riverside Gardens project, and, although the war supervened, Sir Henry finally, in autumn 1971, ended up surveying the shenanigans at the Council House. *(Author)*

Left: Various pet 'development' projects of the city council have pecked away at the original extent and form of the Riverside Gardens, not least the building of the new Crown Court of 1991. Therefore, in 1989 Sir Henry was offered free to Rolls-Royce and fetched up in Victory Road, Sinfin, outside the colossal modernist offices of the firm (by Maxwell Fry, Jane Drew & Partners) where he still stands. Where will he go next, one wonders? *(Author)*

Royal Crown Derby factory, photographed by W. Morrell, 1936. In 1839 a site next to the Arboretum was selected to erect a Union Workhouse for Derby and Litchurch, then two separate local authorities. The architect was John Mason of Derby (1794–1847). In 1877 a new larger workhouse was opened on Uttoxeter Road, and the old one acquired by the newly founded Crown Derby Company ('Royal' only from 1889), keen to make fine china in Derby. In 1878–9 it was adapted by H.I. Stevens's former partner, Frederick Josias Robinson (1834–92), who added the fine portico and tower with a cast-aluminium corona – one of the earliest architectural uses of this metal in the UK. *(Author)*

The factory, January 2004. The factory (which ensured the continuity of china-making in Derby by taking over the King Street factory in 1935) was acquired by Royal Doulton in 1969. The company immediately pulled down the centrepiece and replaced it as here, retaining the cupola, which was refurbished in the 1980s (L). Subsequently, UPVC windows have done Mason's surviving structure no favours aesthetically, but the firm is now independent again under the management of the Hon. Hugh Gibson and the chairmanship of Roger Boissier CBE. *(Peter Billson)*

Osmaston Road, photographed by Messrs W.W. Winter of Midland Road, south, from outside Wilderslow (II), in early afternoon on a hot summer day in 1911. An open-topped electric tram heads for the town centre, with the ornately Gothic Melbourne House (II) on the right, built in 1863–4 for Alderman Robert Pegg, the paint manufacturer; the architect was Thomas Chambers Hine of Nottingham (1813–99). The area was then an extremely fashionable early Victorian suburb, until 1879 part of the autonomous Litchurch. *(Author)*

The scene is remarkably little changed in nearly a century. It is late morning on a hot summer day and the view suffers from being unable to match the depth of field of that preceding. Melbourne House has been much mauled internally and neglected externally thanks to having been acquired by the NHS. All the other villas in the earlier view are still in place, albeit most in very run-down condition, being either in multiple occupancy or split as offices; almost all those prominent chimney pots have gone, thanks to central heating. *(Author)*

The Spot, probably photographed by Charles Barrow Keene, January 1911. This was before the remodelling of the corner, marked by the rear of Queen Victoria, left. The range on the right was built in the 1790s as private houses, and adapted as shops in the mid- to late nineteenth century, McCann's Piano & Organ Saloon (right) being a particularly bravura example. Next to it is the Queen's Vaults Inn, shortly to close for ever. The sign on the left reads 'Public telephone'. *(Derby Museum)*

It took until 1934 to replace The Spot corner building (see bottom picture on p. 79) and a year later the east side of Osmaston Road, as here, was replaced in a similar (but much less well-handled) style, more reminiscent of a north London shopping parade than the centre of an important county borough. The 'gun emplacement' hides most of the St Peter's Street buildings, but most have been replaced since 1911. *(Author)*

5

New Normanton, Burton Road & Littleover

Normanton Road looking north from near the Normanton Hotel, 1905. Most of the private houses built along this road in the 1860s and 1870s have had their front gardens filled in with showroom extensions to turn them into shops; those on the left (note their splendidly ornate ironwork, all ripped out for the war effort in 1942) were treated after this view was taken. The two churches behind electric tram no. 14 were (nearest) the Congregational chapel of 1884 by John Edward Smith (1835–89) – son of the architect of North Parade, now secularised – and Rose Hill Methodist chapel of 1875 by Wesleyan specialist John Wills (1846–1906), demolished in 1989. *(Don Gwinnett)*

Opposite, above: GIs of the US 82nd Airborne Division walk down Normanton Road towards Mill Hill Lane, 1944. Normanton Road developed from a country lane in the 1860s and was widened in 1938–9 when Herbert Aslin built this extension to Derby Technical College (founded in Green Lane in 1878) on an awkward site, already in college occupation but home to a works redundant since 1924. As with the Council House, the outbreak of war prevented its completion to plan. A four-storey L-shaped block, its height artfully broken by an attic cornice, was built almost next to Christ Church. A potentially handsome southward curving extension of twenty-five bays never got beyond the ground floor, and when money did become available a new start was made on Kedleston Road, now the university. (Derby Evening Telegraph)

Opposite, below: The university (founded from disparate elements, including the technical college in 1992) declared Aslin's building redundant in 1996, and it was sold to developers Wheatcroft, who planned to create a retail park there. However, Mr Clinton Bourke, representing the developer, soon fell out with the council, his scheme twice rejected on planning grounds. Unfortunately, by this time the college had been peremptorily demolished. The surviving building is the 1950s Ministry of Pensions offices. Christ Church (II), sadly shorn of its pinnacles, is now Serbian Orthodox. *(Author)*

For some obscure reason Mr Bourke spared two of Aslin's elegant Classical entrance aedicules, both beautifully detailed, although this one – once the main entrance to the building – has lost the octagonal pediment urns that terminated the pilasters. Note the immaculate brickwork, laid to Flemish bond; what builder can do that today? Whether to stay or be sold, they remain, mournful reminders of the spectacular curving arcade they once embellished. The site, with its ugly hoardings, continues to moulder and the dispute to fester, a truly lamentable situation. *(Author)*

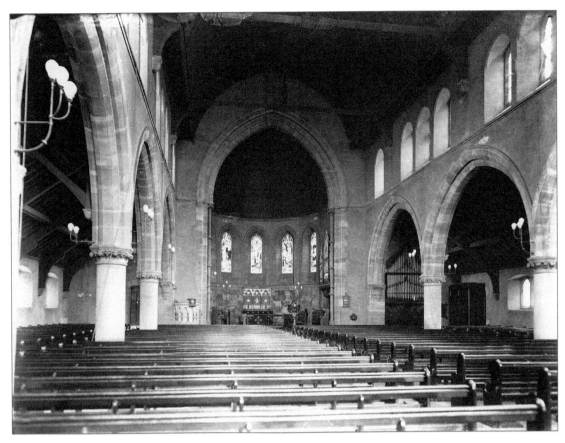

Opposite, above: St Chad's Church, photographed by Keene, 1899. As this part of New Normanton expanded churches were built. St Chad's named the road it stood upon at the junction of Mount Carmel Street with Gordon Road, where also stood the Catholic Church of St Joseph of 1897 by James Hart. St Chad's was built in 1882, the competition to design it being won by H.C. Turner. Here St Chad's unexpectedly effective apsed interior, complete with Edwin Haslam gas brackets, is seen. *(Author)*

Opposite, below: The exterior of St Chad's, photographed from Mount Carmel Street by Keene, 1899. Behind the church are the schools and on the left is St Joseph's (since the 1970s the Polish Catholic Church of St Maksymilian Kolbe). *(Author)*

The chancel of St Chad's, just before the church closed for demolition, 1990. The whole apse to sill level is lined with Chellaston alabaster installed by R.G. Lomas & Co. of King Street marble works (see bottom picture on p. 45). The wrought-iron supports for the communion rail were by Edwin Haslam. The demolition was prompted by the vicar, believing they could sell most of the site to fund a smaller church on a remnant. Needless to say, this did not happen and what's left of the congregation now meets in a school room. A fine church was needlessly destroyed. *(Mrs T.W. Fraser)*

Richmond Laundry, Clarence Road, Normanton, 1909. In 1908 Charles Frederick Pritchard, scion of a family long involved in the manufacture of both brushes and soft drinks, chose a location in Clarence Road to which to move his Richmond Gold Medal Laundry. He had Alexander MacPherson of Derby (1847–1935) design this handsome brick building, which remained in dedicated use until the 1990s. *(Private Collection)*

The interior of the rear top-lit workshop at the Richmond Laundry 1908. Laundering was a very labour-intensive industry, a fact strikingly borne out here. The mangles were driven by a steam engine, the chimney of which can be seen rising up behind the front offices in the photograph above. *(Private Collection)*

When the Richmond Laundry Works finally closed in 1999 they were bought by a local man who allowed the building to fall into some disrepair. However, the councillor for the area was positively ecstatic at having persuaded him to demolish the complex to build houses on the site – on the grounds that the building had become a danger to children playing (i.e. trespassing!) – despite the fact that it could so easily and attractively have been adapted as flats, or even 'prestige apartments'. Work on demolition began on 13 January 2004, when this photograph was taken. What a waste of a good building! *(Author)*

Belvoir Street, New Normanton, *c.* 1907. Originally intended by the developer, Joseph Porter of Spondon, to be called Lumley Street (after the castle and surname of the Earls of Scarbrough – hardly redolent with local associations), it and several neighbouring streets were eventually named after local hunts. Just out of view on the right is the Mafeking & Bowling Green Inn, with a date-stone of 1900, thus dating the street, which runs from Porter Road (which the developer named after himself) to Clarence Road. *(Michael Allseybrook Esq.)*

Belvoir Street, 2001. The houses are identical in plan, layout and detail to those in Porter Road, except that those in the latter are all terraced, whereas here they are all but four in semi-detached pairs. They have sprouted satellite TV aerials, UPVC windows, 'Kentucky' doors (also in UPVC) and motor cars. The iron railings on their dwarf brick walls were ripped out for the war effort in 1942, and now are mainly replaced by reconstituted stone. The vacant ground in the foreground of the previous picture was dedicated in 1908 to the Clarence Road Schools (now Dale Primary), designed by the Belper firm of Hunter & Woodhouse. A remarkably handsome design, it has been ruined in the last twenty years by poorly designed and unsightly extensions. *(Carole Craven)*

Opposite, above: Littleover Grange. Littleover is but a short pitch up the Burton Road from Clarence Road, and The Grange (L), from 1939 until 1971 an outpost of Rolls-Royce (adding a huge wing), was always thought of as a rather pedestrian early Victorian villa. However, a sale of drawings in October 2003 established that this house was in fact designed by Lewis Cottingham (1787–1847) and built in 1818–19 for John Harrison, an opulent Derby attorney. There were fourteen drawings in all for Harrison's villa, representing seven projects, this one being closest to the design adopted. *(Mellors & Kirk)*

Opposite, below: Littleover Grange, August 1982. The house was built but with slight differences, such as paired columns at each end of the veranda and altered chimneys. Harrison himself decided by 1826 to go and live in the vast Gothic pile Cottingham had built for him at Snelston, and in 1874 iron founder Reuben Eastwood bought it, adding a wing with a campanile on the north (entrance) side, a pair of canted bays on the south and replacing all the windows with plate glass; he also filled in the central niche. The room at the top of the tower, it is said, was to enable Eastwood to contemplate the fires of his foundry while enjoying a glass of port and a Havana after dinner. *(Author)*

In 1972 the Derbyshire Freemasons acquired the house, but it unfortunately burnt down on 2 December 1990, with the loss of their collections going back to the eighteenth century as well as some fine interiors. Subsequently it was rebuilt a bay wider each side of the veranda on the garden front, with UPVC windows and no chimneys. *(Author)*

Littleover Old Hall (L) always seems a misnomer for this elegant Arts and Crafts house built in 1898 for Edward MacInnes to a design of Alexander MacPherson's (see top picture on p. 96). After many vicissitudes – between 1954 and 71 it was yet another Rolls-Royce outpost – most of the parkland was sold for development and it became the Fire Service HQ, although in November 2003 was on the market for the second time in three years. *(Derbyshire Fire & Rescue Service)*

Littleover Old Hall, watercolour by 'H.H.' (Harpur Heathcote of Littleover) after J. Rolfe, 1873. The name derived from the house's predecessor, built, conceivably by John Smythson, for Sir Richard Harpur (died 1633). It started out as a mini-Hardwick, but by the time of this painting it had been reduced to two eighteenth-century brick ranges and two remaining Jacobean towers, and was a farm tenanted under the Heathcotes, the Harpurs' successors. Within a decade even the towers were gone and it was finally demolished in 1897. *(Derbyshire Fire & Rescue Service)*

Burton Road, not long after the tram route was electrified, 8 September 1904. From Littleover one returns to Derby via Burton Road which, on its final descent, passes Mount Carmel, an elevated residential enclave built on the grounds of a long-vanished house. The villas lining Burton Road here date from the late 1880s and many are by Arthur Eaton, including the one with the turret (right). Beyond it is the Moorish Mount Carmel Tower of 1869, actually the chimney of Messrs Mason's paint works. It was designed by Edwin Thompson (1801–83). *(Michael Allseybrook Esq.)*

The scene is not much changed, for once, except that not long after this photograph was taken the paint works closed and Mount Carmel Tower came down, to be replaced after the First World War by a motor garage. On the left, three villas have been connected together (to no good aesthetic effect) to create the International Hotel, which has been growing since its foundation in the 1950s. The turning, centre, is Breedon Hill Road, pitched in 1894. *(Author)*

Windmill Pit, photographed by Keene, early 1860s. Windmill Pit may be the same as the 'ordeal pit' mentioned in a charter of 1160; otherwise it is first mentioned in 1553, three years before the Protestant martyr Joan Wast was burnt there for heresy on 1 August. Another execution is known from 1602, thereafter the Pit – associated with the mill (demolished August 1816) that gave Mill Hill Lane its name – is mentioned up until 1881. The land on the far side of the fence is that of Mill Hill House, with Mill Hill Lane out of view beyond. *(Derby Museum)*

In view of the Pit's associations, it is surprising that no church organisation has bought the site and dedicated it as somewhere a little special. Between 1898 and 1902 Lime Avenue was pitched into the Pit, ending in a turn-round against a sheer wall, seen here. Fine Edwardian houses were built, a few interwar bungalows and some recent housing association flats replacing a pair of villas. Yet there is no commemorative plaque to poor Joan nor any other reminder anywhere on site. *(Author)*

Burton Road, Little City, *c.* 1909. Little City was a very small enclave of some of the worst houses in Derby, situated at the top of Green Lane and built in about 1815. That part of it facing Burton Road, however, was more respectable, as seen here on the right, including part of the Tailors' Arms which, like the area itself, survived until 1960. Here the Normanton Road joins (left) and both continue behind the photographer down Babington Lane to The Spot; to the right is Green Lane, previously Green Hill. Also on the left is Alexander MacPherson's Unity House (for the Derby TUC, 1908) and a fine iron *pissoir*. *(Michael Allseybrook Esq.)*

The loss of Little City enabled Burton Road to be widened (right) and the layout massaged by traffic engineers. The stuccoed building in the distance (just visible beyond the tram, above) is the Bell & Castle Inn (II) of 1801 and still going strong. Unity House was demolished (to a tide of indifference from the local trades' unions who had sold it long before) in 1989 and replaced by a combined GP surgery and retail pharmacy. One of M. Decaux's spaceships has replaced the much handier *pissoir*. *(Author)*

Green Lane, *c.* 1905. In 1851 Nottingham architect Thomas Chambers Hine was asked to design three of what would today be described as 'prestige homes' on land belonging to the Revd Roseingrave Macklin, vicar of Christ Church. One was 1 (later 73) Wilson Street, the others 110–12 Green Lane (all II). The design was in Hine's best 'Fantasy Jacobethan' mode. *(Author)*

The interiors of these houses were fairly lavish. No. 73 was owned by James Harwood (1841–1925), a Colchester-born stationer who founded his Derby shop in 1864. This view of the staircase hall was in the sale catalogue of the contents held on 23 June 1925 after his death; he was a prodigious collector. Note the mid-eighteenth-century John Whitehurst FRS angle barometer (right) and the fact that the interiors were entirely Classical. *(Author)*

After the First World War this area ceased to be fashionable, and these houses were divided up, first as flats and then, after the Second World War, as office space. The two houses that comprised 110–12 Green Lane were sold in 2002 as office premises. Externally, though, little has changed in eighty years, whereas the interiors have been badly mauled, with the loss of cornicing, fireplaces and other details. *(Author)*

The Primitive Methodist Chapel, photographed by Keene, 1896. From this point upwards to Babington Lane, what today is Green Lane was until a century ago called Green Hill. This Italianate chapel was built in 1878 for the 'Prims' by Giles & Brookhouse of Derby. The strange thing is that it is an exact copy of the same partnership's long demolished Bourne chapel in Kedleston Street, in Derby's old West End, built eight years before, presumably at the insistence of the Green Hill congregation. *(Author)*

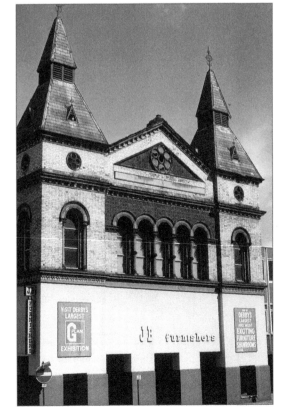

In the twentieth century the 'Prims' were reabsorbed by the Methodist movement, and by 1967 a dwindling and ageing congregation caused the sale of the premises. The purchaser was the proprietor of JB Furnishers, purveyors of 'G-plan' to the unsuspecting masses. In adapting the building, wholesale slaughter of the interior and the mauling of the lower part of the exterior were apparently necessary. The original 'Prims' would no doubt be turning in their graves if they knew that the building was currently a so-called amusement arcade. This photograph was taken in September 1975. *(Author)*

6

Victoria Street to Ashbourne Road

St James's Street from across Victoria Street, with the corporation's 1950s' roundabout with its cement 'basket of flowers' and artful planting, 1963. To the left are The Strand and The Wardwick. All the buildings visible except the GPO (right) are by Giles & Brookhouse, 1869–77. The culverted brook runs beneath the road just the other side of the roundabout. 'Connecting Derby' has cleared this area of traffic at the cost of plastering the street scene with reconstituted stone paviours and brushed aluminium Modernist-kitsch street furniture. (Author)

Victoria Street decorated for a state visit by Queen Victoria, 21 May 1891. The street was created by the culverting of the Markeaton Brook in 1837–9. On the right is Robert Wallace's 1839 Athenaeum (II); ahead, just visible through the pouring rain, is the bulk of T.C. Hine's Brookside (Congregational) chapel of 1860. The lavish street adornments were funded by the Mayor, maritime refrigeration pioneer Sir Alfred Seale Haslam, knighted that morning on platform one of Derby station. *(Derby Museum)*

Victoria Street, June 2004. The Athenaeum is still there, despite conversion in 1950 into DHSS offices and re-conversion into a catering facility in 1987. The whole south side in the previous photograph has been pulled down and replaced by the serpentine façade of Ranby's store of 1962, now Debenham's. Hine's chapel went as part of the Ranby's scheme in 1961, a replacement chapel being provided within the new development, just visible behind the 'To Let' board, right. The obtrusive roadworks (in their twenty-fifth month in September 2004) are the outward and visible sign of the inward and visible disgrace that is 'Connecting Derby'. *(Author)*

St James's Bridge, photographed by Keene before 1869, when St James's Lane (right) was widened. Greater precision is not possible, as none of the commercial premises named seem to appear at this address in any directory between 1852 and 1870. The stone bridge spans the Markeaton Brook, culverted before it and open beyond. It was designed by William Strutt FRS (1756–1831), replacing a timber one mentioned by William Woolley in about 1712, where the monks of the Cell of St James levied a toll before the Dissolution. *(Derby Museum)*

St James's area, 1907. In 1877–8 the brook was culverted to create The Strand (right). The corner building (II) was built in 1878–9, and those lining The Strand (II) in 1879–80, all by Giles & Brookhouse. The spire (centre left) is that of the Museum & Art Gallery (II). *(Author)*

In this 2003 scene the former General Post Office (II), right, contrasts favourably with the Giles & Brookhouse buildings. The GPO was designed by J. Williams (the GPO architect of the day) and built in 1869–71, being extended in St James's Street in 1873. In 2003 the post office, having been vacated in 2000, was adapted into a drinking establishment called Coyote Wild. This has given the building a future, but has done it no favours, the exterior being festooned with vast inappropriate signs, up- and downlighters and other clutter, all added without listed building or conservation area consent. Note the semi-permanent mess. *(Author)*

St James's Street, Sunday 22 May 1932. This was the worst flood since that of 1841 and, although there was no loss of life, millions of pounds of damage was caused, for most businesses then stored their stock in cellarage. The flood was caused – as Herbert Spencer had realised at the tender age of twenty in 1841 – by water backing up the swollen Derwent from the Trent and into the Markeaton Brook, itself in torrent. His solution – a movable barrier at Alvaston – was not accepted by the council until 1933, a wait of ninety-two years! *(Private Collection)*

St James's Street, May 2002. The street has been half pedestrianised since 1992. The three-storey building is the former St James's Hotel (II), designed by Giles & Brookhouse and opened in 1871. It closed in about 1925–6, leaving just a part of its ground floor as a series of bars and a (then) good restaurant. The ballroom became (until 1990) Richardson & Linell's auction rooms. The bar still remains (from 2002 as Sugaz) but the remainder is split as offices. *(Author)*

No. 21 The Wardwick, a previously unknown print by Keene. This building has now been replaced by the Susumi sushibar. On the right is the 1708 former Allsopp town house, now the Wardwick Tavern. Although it has been difficult to determine much of its history, its elegant proportions and lack of detailing strongly suggest Joseph Pickford in his later years, *c.* 1778–82. The fact that the first floor clearly has the loftiest rooms suggests it was intended as a town house. From 1852 to 1878 it was home to solicitor Henry H. Hutchinson. *(Author)*

The same view today, with no. 21 replaced by a much taller commercial building in the style of Giles & Brookhouse and erected in about 1879 for the Linnells, drapers. The still lofty first-floor room was the County Club (see top picture on p. 121) for a long time, but after a long tenure by Golden Gains it became Susumi. No. 19/20 (Wardwick Tavern) has clearly had its shop fronting of the 1860s replaced by sash windows. *(Author)*

This superb town house of 1611 is shown in an architectural elevation of 1852 drawn by John Price of Derby. Innovatively designed, with much horizontal use of glass, it was long the residence of the Gisborne family, passing in the eighteenth century to the Heathcotes of Littleover Old Hall who sold it to Alderman Francis Jessopp. It had 2 acres of formal gardens watered by the Bramble Brook, a Gothic stable block and a Bakewell Gate. *(Derby Museum)*

In 1966 the Jacobean House, long a café, closed, was asset-stripped and converted into an estate agency. The stable block was summarily demolished and the remaining garden was given over to the construction of an enormous office block (looming darkly above the house, left of centre) with a multi-storey car park beyond. The ground-floor windows were drastically dropped (fairly tactfully) and glazed, giving the house transoms where none had ever originally been intended. Since 2002 it has been a café-bar called The Haus (surely Das Haus?). The photograph was taken from the author's office window at the museum in May 1993. *(Author)*

Opposite, below: Jessopp's house, photographed by Keene, 1881. In the time of Alderman Jessopp's son, F.J. Jessopp, the borough council decided it wanted to pitch a road from Macklin Street to Wardwick. This would necessitate the removal of three-fifths of Jessopp's house. He therefore had John Price draw the house and make plans before truncating it and re-erecting a new side elevation from the salvaged materials. He employed Augustus Oakley Deacon (1819–99) to make paintings of all the main rooms, so the house would be fully recorded. *(Author)*

St Werburgh's Church (B), platinotype by Keene, 1880s. This Saxon foundation, originally set within a small settlement called Wardwick but part of Derby by 1086, has had a chequered history. The medieval tower collapsed on 2 January 1601 and was replaced by 1608, as here, in an unaffectedly vernacular Gothic way. In 1698 most of the medieval nave collapsed and was replaced by the elegant Baroque church seen here. The nave was top-lit by a dome, but the architect is not known for sure. Note the cabbies' rest (right) in Cheapside. *(Author)*

St Werburgh's, 1938. In 1894 the church was again declared unsafe, and the nave was replaced by a new, Gothic one on a non-liturgical alignment (to help obviate undermining by flooding), designed by Sir Arthur Blomfield (1829–99) and finished in 1898. The elegant Regency Neo-Greek cast-iron railings visible here survived, but all bar a couple of panels were removed to build iron Spitfires in 1942. The chancel was also left intact, with its chantry monument, now in the care of the Churches Conservation Trust; the remainder, secularised in 1982 and briefly a shopping mall, has been derelict for thirteen years. *(Private Collection)*

The chancel of St Werburgh's Church, 1938. This was completed with the dedication of the carved reredos and royal arms by Henry Huss (died 1716). The brass lectern was originally a font which lived beneath an ogiform iron cover by Robert Bakewell. A nineteenth-century vicar turned the former into a lectern and had a banal stone font made to go with the cover.

The chancel has a hipped roof, unlike the nave, which was parapeted, making one think that the two were separate builds, although the exterior order was the same and the detailing generally similar. *(Private Collection)*

Sir Arthur Blomfield's nave looking to the liturgical east (actually north) during work to convert it into a shopping mall, July 1989. Note the superb oak screen, stained glass by Kempe and wrought-iron communion rail by Edwin Haslam. The mall went bankrupt in 1993, and the church has been derelict for more than a decade. Dr Johnson married Tetty Porter at this church on 9 July 1735. *(Author)*

King's Arms County Hotel (II), a newly discovered Keene photograph, probably of 1877. This four-square hotel was added to the Shire Hall complex for the convenience of attorneys, plaintiffs and others attending the assizes. It was probably designed by the Improvement Commission's architect, Charles Finney (1773–1828), and was finished in 1798, the sheriff's officer, John Webster, being the proprietor.

On his death it was extended in matching style. In this picture its 'Derby' windows (sashes paired under a single stone lintel) have already been reglazed in plate glass and the parapet rebuilt.

The mystery is what it was like originally – the work was advertised as 'recent' in December 1876. *(Michael J. Willis Esq.)*

Below: The building was turned into a library by the county council (which removed both original staircases and blocked the street entrance) in 1934 and a police station in 1968, closing in 1988. It, the Shire Hall and the Judges' Lodgings – all part of a single superbly elegant complex – were then allowed to become derelict from 1994. Plans to convert the lot into thirteen magistrates' courts (far too many for such a complex) included the complete demolition of this building, but a vigorous campaign by Derby Civic Society against such destructive plans resulted in a reprieve, and it was adapted as part of the new courts (with a huge and ugly extension behind) in 2002–3. *(Author)*

King's Arms County Hotel, August 1990. This view of the hotel shows it in a state of dereliction. The county council had destroyed its austere symmetry by removing the chimneys, raising two attic windows and inserting a new one at bay two. That, combined with damp, plant growth and vandalism, made it extremely difficult to 'sell' as a candidate for retention. *(Author)*

Below: Today its restoration vindicates all the threats and unpleasantness directed at those fighting this building's corner. It looks just right and satisfyingly complements the Shire Hall (see picture on p. 13) and Judges' Lodgings. The stucco royal arms inn sign, stone gates and cast-iron railings of 1826 have also been restored. Indeed, the lavish amounts of money poured into renovating the historic elements probably explains the awfulness of the new build, which hardly enhances the Grade I listed Shire Hall nor makes up for the loss of Matthew Habershon's demolished extensions. *(Author)*

Theatre Royal, Bold Lane, sepia print by Samuel Hereford Parkins, after 1884. Very few satisfactory views of this interesting building survive before its façade of 1773 (attributed to Joseph Pickford for James Whiteley) was terribly mauled by that bastion of art and culture, Derbyshire County Council. After 1864 it was turned by Alderman Wilkins (a Dissenting printer) into a gospel hall. Compared with a very eccentric engraving of 1791, it stands up well. The building was, in fact, a conversion of a maltings. *(Derby Museum, Goodey Collection No. 157)*

After the war the gospel hall failed to retain its appeal and it was sold to the county council, who adapted it first as a library and later as magistrates' courts. While this undoubtedly saved it, it meant that the original (reportedly ornate) interior was entirely stripped out and that the façade was wrecked. The upper windows were dropped through the sill band to the plat band, the arcade was plastered in and something akin to shop-fronting installed. In 2003 it became redundant and is for sale. Planning permission has been applied for to turn it into storage or into a comedy club, and a local group (lacking funding) would like to turn it into a studio theatre. The county council just want the money. *(Author)*

A 1712 drawing of Lower Friar Gate. This house was inhabited in her widowhood by Mrs Thomas Parker, mother of sleazy Lord Chancellor Thomas, 1st Earl of Macclesfield (1666–1732), who was both Recorder of Derby from 1703 to 1710 and the Borough's MP. The house was clearly timber framed and jettied, and by 1712 it had been divided into four tenements and a butcher's shop (right) with rear access. In 1831 Stephen Glover claimed that it was 'taken down some years ago'. *(Author)*

Both the interiors and the rear of this whole line of properties (11½ to 15½ Friar Gate) are very ancient, replete with unexpected gables, tanked-in newel staircases, altered fenestration and other un-Georgian elements. Mrs Parker's house was clearly re-fronted into about three separate buildings; the rainwater hopper nearest the camera carries the date 1806, which about fits the date. These properties badly need listing. *(Author)*

An illustration of The Friary (II) by E. Trowell on a Royal Crown Derby plate, part of the 1887 Boden service presented by the employees of Boden's (lace) Mill on the occasion of the marriage of Henry Boden's son Walter, 8 May 1888. Henry Boden had acquired The Friary from the Mozleys in the 1860s, enlarging it to designs by Frederick Josias Robinson and Alexander MacPherson. The 16 acres of grounds were reduced somewhat by his philanthropical urge to provide housing. The house had been built for Samuel Crompton in 1731, probably to a design by Richard Jackson of Armitage and enlarged by his son in 1760. Much of the interior is still very fine. *(Mellors & Kirk)*

Mrs Henry Boden was a great Temperance campaigner, so when she sold up in 1921 she was horrified to learn that The Friary had been turned into a (licensed) hotel. It was progressively enlarged from the 1960s, losing the last of its land to the erection of Heritage Gate. It was in the hands of the official receiver in the 1990s and is now a Bass (hotel) management residential training establishment – unwelcoming of visitors although it doubles as a 'fun pub' called It's a Scream – the sign until recently being a copy of Edvard Munch's *The Scream*. *(Author)*

No. 103 Friar Gate, 1963.
The Portland Temperance Club was in residence here until 1922, when, as a result of the loss of financial support from the widowed Mrs Boden of The Friary, who moved to Chard, the club was forced to move out. The County Club, which had been housed at 21 The Wardwick, bought it after this. Before the 1890s it had been a private house, a very severe Regency building with a façade full of Derby windows, much like the King's Arms County Hotel (see pictures on pp. 116–17), and it may thus be tentatively attributed to Charles Finney and dated to about 1795–1800. *(Don Farnsworth)*

In 1971–2 the club and the 1694 Presbyterian chapel next door were demolished in order to clear space for a vast and inappropriate office development by T.H. Thorpe & Partners sponsored by Viking Properties and mockingly called Heritage Gate, most of which remained untenanted for well over a decade. The promoters were rather bailed out when the city council acquired Roman House – the part on the site of the County Club – in 1988. The four-storey street front here is in a banal sub-Georgian pastiche with an ersatz Doric portico representing what can politely be called a playful use of the orders. The building in the background, in Stafford Street, has recently been ear-marked for demolition; the street is to be incorporated into 'Connecting Derby'. *(Author)*

Friar Gate railway bridge, 1948. This photograph, part of a batch of unknown provenance that was rescued from a skip, shows the west side of this railway bridge. The line was built by the Great Northern Railway in 1876–8, and the ornate bridge by Andrew Handyside & Co. of Duke Street was a trade-off to meet residents' objections. It is actually two bridges, each one carrying a double track, side by side. Here the signal gantry seems ridiculously obtrusive. Note the street furniture still bearing blackout stripes. The station entrance was up the turning on the right. *(Author)*

The station closed to passengers from 7 September 1964 and the line altogether three years later. The tracks were lifted, signal gantry removed, the station partly converted into a used car emporium (hence the scruffy sign board seen here) and the bridge was eventually sold to the city council for £1. A huge residential development on the site of the station and goods yard is expected to go ahead. There are five houses on the left of Georgian origin, but three were given ugly Victorian fenestration. A current restoration scheme has unwisely extended this disfigurement to the rest. *(Author)*

Bridge Street, 1887. This building was built as a result of the First Derby Improvement Act of 1768, and is attributable to the architect Joseph Pickford (II). It is two houses, a two-bay one facing Friar Gate (left) and a three-bay south-facing one – seen here decorated for Queen Victoria's Golden Jubilee in 1887 – its offset entrance reached through a garden to the side facing the camera. The Third Improvement Act, however, which allowed the sale of Nuns' Green, resulted in the pitching of Bridge Street through it in 1793, putting the entrance virtually on the pavement. *(Private Collection)*

The same scene in February 2004. Little has changed, except that the house was altered for two surgeons in 1900 to designs by Percy Currey. The rear extension, probably erected in 1793, has had a modest ground-floor part added to a canted stair tower placed where the extension joins the house, and the entrance has been rebuilt with an Ionic portico, one side of which is supported by a rusticated pillar. Modern plumbing has marred the well-proportioned façade and the elegant plain railings of 1793 were ripped up in 1942. The road outside, now part of a one-way system, is like a race track – surely no way to treat your premier conservation area. *(Author)*

Vernon Street, September 1990. The county gaol, built in lowering Doric by Francis Goodwin in 1826, was closed 102 years later and the interior buildings cleared to make way for a dog track. The surviving screen walls and grand entrance were useful security as well as an excellent disguise for the tin-roofed stands (just visible on the right) and other paraphernalia needed to race greyhounds. The track closed a few years before 1990, and after Mr Lawson's depression had killed off a disastrous plan to build a 36-storey tower here, a more modest proposal prevailed. *(Author)*

Vernon Street, March 2000. One benefit of the final scheme, called Vernon Gate – showing that the Norse suffix for street has millennium-long staying power – was that the entrance was handsomely refurbished, after having been in decay for seventy years. Unfortunately, the mixed office and residential development inside was built in a gimcrack style with no relationship to the façade whatsoever. All the other high brick curtain walls – unadorned, severe, yet grand and still able to provide excellent security – were removed, along with two surviving bastions to the west. Nevertheless, the street scene as the powerful visual termination of any view along Vernon Street has been immeasurably improved. *(Author)*

Ashbourne Road, *c.* 1909. This is looking west from the corner of Fowler Street; note the impressive row of middling quality Regency villas that line the north side, no. 28 being nearest the camera. Almost behind the tramway catenary support, centre, is the oddly designed no. 39, with no. 40, home of that indefatigable patron of Derby topographical art, Alfred E. Goodey (1869–1945), beyond. *(Private Collection)*

Taken from a point slightly further up (halfway between Fowler Street and Slater Avenue, left) this view apparently shows little change in June 2004. The porticoed villa nos 32–4 has long been the Georgian House Hotel, with part clumsily adapted as a pub, opened in 1996 as Mr Grundy's. At the time of writing, the gap between it and no. 39 is going to be filled with a substantial block of flats, with no. 39 itself converted into four apartments. Goodey's house is now a nursery, and further down another villa has been replaced by a filling station. The modern railing to the left shields The Cedars, a villa that dates from about 1770 by James Denstone for the Curzons, later the home of founder Andrew Handyside and now a development company's HQ. *(Author)*

Ashbourne Road, 1906. Ensconced in his pram at the corner of Surrey Street and Ashbourne Road is eleven-month-old Bill, son of Frederick William Gilbert (1866–1941), of a family long resident in Clifton House, behind (centre). Behind the boy (left) is Colville Street, with the chapel-like Wesleyan Schools on the corner (see below) and the stabling of Stretton's Manchester brewery between that and the Gilberts' home. The building just visible (right) is the Ashbourne Road Wesleyan chapel of 1878 (extended 1885), designed by Methodist master-builder John Wills. *(Frank Gilbert)*

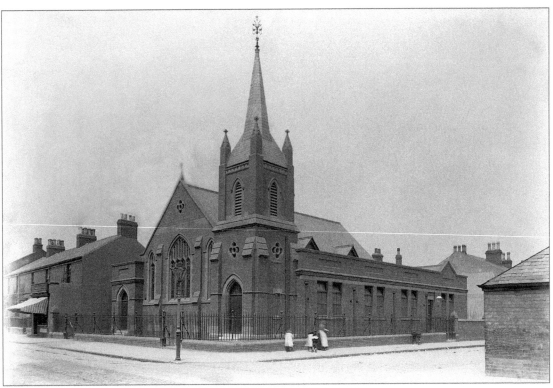

Ninety-five years later Bill Gilbert's great-granddaughter Isobel (aged thirteen months) poses for the camera in the same spot, January 2001. Clifton House and the brewery stables have become a filling station and the Methodist chapel was demolished in 1986. *(Frank Gilbert)*

Opposite, below: The Wesleyan Schools building on the corner of Colville Street, photographed by Keene when it had just been completed in 1901, again to the designs of the ubiquitous Wills. It was replaced by a joint Methodist and United Reformed Church (URC) chapel in 1999. *(Author)*

Mickleover Old Hall, 1880s. This was built as a two-pile small manor house by a Parliamentary officer of yeoman stock called Robert Cotchett (1611–57), and is dated both 1648 and 1653 inside. His grandson Thomas started the first Derby silk mill in 1702, but on his death in 1713 it was bought by the Newtons, lords of the manor, and converted into a farm. In 1816 Alderman Samuel Rowland, an agronomist, built Mickleover House nearby and acquired the Old Hall, which he renamed Cedar Lodge and used as a gardener's cottage, a role it still fulfilled when this photograph was taken. *(Don Gwinnett)*

After the Second World War Edward Gothard reduced Mickleover House, and sold the lodge, the stable block (thereafter Overfields) and the Old Hall as separate freeholds, and suddenly the house – one of the very few timber-framed houses of any pretension within the city – became a desirable property. Refurbished, shorn of its Victorian bargeboards (but not of its Regency cast-iron casements) and sensitively restored, it has become a favourite with senior executives posted to local companies and has changed hands several times within the last thirty years. *(Author)*